FLOYD CLYMER'S MOTORCYCLIST'S LIBRARY

The Book of the
TRIUMPH TWINS

A comprehensive and practical guide to the proper handling and maintenance of 1956–69 twin-cylinder spring frame models except 1967–9 models T100T, T120R and T150 (Trident)

W. C. Haycraft

ANNOUNCEMENT

By special arrangement with the original publishers of this book, Sir Isaac Pitman & Son, Ltd., of London, England, we have secured the exclusive publishing rights for this book, as well as all others in THE MOTORCYCLIST'S LIBRARY.

Included in THE MOTORCYCLIST'S LIBRARY are complete instruction manuals covering the care and operation of respective motorcycles and engines; valuable data on speed tuning, and thrilling accounts of motorcycle race events. See listing of available titles elsewhere in this edition.

We consider it a privilege to be able to offer so many fine titles to our customers.

FLOYD CLYMER
Publisher of Books Pertaining to Automobiles and Motorcycles
2125 W. PICO ST.   LOS ANGELES 6, CALIF.

INTRODUCTION

Welcome to the world of digital publishing ~ the book you now hold in your hand, while unchanged from the original edition, was printed using the latest state of the art digital technology. The advent of print-on-demand has forever changed the publishing process, never has information been so accessible and it is our hope that this book serves your informational needs for years to come. If this is your first exposure to digital publishing, we hope that you are pleased with the results. Many more titles of interest to the classic automobile and motorcycle enthusiast, collector and restorer are available via our website at www.VelocePress.com. We hope that you find this title as interesting as we do.

NOTE FROM THE PUBLISHER

The information presented is true and complete to the best of our knowledge. All recommendations are made without any guarantees on the part of the author or the publisher, who also disclaim all liability incurred with the use of this information.

TRADEMARKS

We recognize that some words, model names and designations, for example, mentioned herein are the property of the trademark holder. We use them for identification purposes only. This is not an official publication.

INFORMATION ON THE USE OF THIS PUBLICATION

This manual is an invaluable resource for the classic motorcycle enthusiast and a "must have" for owners interested in performing their own maintenance. However, in today's information age we are constantly subject to changes in common practice, new technology, availability of improved materials and increased awareness of chemical toxicity. As such, it is advised that the user consult with an experienced professional prior to undertaking any procedure described herein. While every care has been taken to ensure correctness of information, it is obviously not possible to guarantee complete freedom from errors or omissions or to accept liability arising from such errors or omissions. Therefore, any individual that uses the information contained within, or elects to perform or participate in do-it-yourself repairs or modifications acknowledges that there is a risk factor involved and that the publisher or its associates cannot be held responsible for personal injury or property damage resulting from the use of the information or the outcome of such procedures.

WARNING!

One final word of advice, this publication is intended to be used as a reference guide, and when in doubt the reader should consult with a qualified technician.

Preface

THIS new edition of Pitman's handbook (thoroughly revised) includes all essential maintenance instructions applicable to 1956–69 350, 500 and 650 c.c. spring-frame Triumph Twins. These machines are—
1. The 1958–66 348 c.c. Twenty-one (Model 3TA).
2. The 1963–68 348 c.c. Tiger 90 (Model T90).
3. The 1956–66 498 c.c. Speed Twins (Models 5T and 5TA).
4. The 1956–69 490 c.c. Tiger 100 (Models T100, T100A and T100S/S).
5. The 1956–66 649 c.c. Thunderbird (Model 6T).
6. The 1956–69 649 c.c. Trophy (Models TR5, TR6 and TR6S/S).
7. The 1956–61 649 c.c. Tiger 110 (Model T110).
8. The 1959–69 649 c.c. Bonneville (Model T120).

The 1968–9 Triumph twins modifications include the following: the fitting of: a different type cylinder head on 1968–9 500 c.c. models; to provision of an oil tank dipstick (1969 only); Amal "Concentric" instead of "Monobloc" type carburettors; an oil-pressure red warning-light on the headlamp top-face (1969 only); improved push-rod cover tubes (1969 only); a slightly modified contact-breaker; a quickly-detachable plug at the rear of the cylinder block for quickly positioning and locking the pistons at T.D.C.; a repositioned Zener diode (beneath the headlamp); an improved hinged side-panel on the nearside; redesigned telescopic front forks; twin-leading-shoe front brakes; a stop-lamp switch incorporated in the front brake linkage (1969 only); and a modified clutch adjustment.

The 1968–9 Triumph twin modifications where not dealt with in detail in the appropriate chapters or sections of this book, are referred to on pages 121–130. In conclusion I sincerely thank the Triumph Engineering Co. Ltd. for assisting me with regard to technical data and for kindly according me permission to reproduce various Triumph copyright illustrations in this handbook. Several motor-cycle accessory firms are also thanked for their helpful co-operation.

W. C. HAYCRAFT

Contents

CHAP.		PAGE
1	HANDLING A TRIUMPH	1
	The controls—Position of controls, etc.—Starting—Running-in—Don't run into trouble!	
2	CORRECT CARBURATION	10
	Amal "Monobloc" carburettor—Tuning "Monobloc" carburettor—Amal carburettor maintenance—The air filter—The S.U. M.C.2 carburettor	
3	TRIUMPH LUBRICATION	24
	Engine lubrication—Motor-cycle lubrication	
4	LIGHTING AND IGNITION SYSTEMS	43
	The Lucas dynamo (1956–59)—The Lucas magneto (1956–59)—Lucas A.C./D.C. lighting and ignition (350, 500 c.c. models)—Lucas energy-transfer ignition and battery charging system—Lucas A.C./D.C. lighting and ignition (350, 500 and 650 c.c. models)—Lucas lamps (1956–69 models)—Lucas battery maintenance—The horn—Sparking plugs	
5	GENERAL MAINTENANCE: THE MOTOR-CYCLE . . .	68
	Cleaning—Forks and steering head—Wheels, brakes, tyres—Chain maintenance—Frame and sidecar hints—The gearbox and clutch	
6	GENERAL MAINTENANCE: THE ENGINE	90
	Valve clearances—Valve timing—Ignition timing—Decarbonizing and grinding-in valves	
	APPENDIX: GENERAL MAINTENANCE (1968–9 Models T90, T100S/S, TR6, T120)	121
	Index	131

1 Handling a Triumph

THOSE who have previously handled other makes of four-stroke motor-cycle should acquire the knack of handling a Triumph almost immediately. But novices should not attempt to ride on the road until they thoroughly understand the layout and use of the various controls.

Taking over the Machine. The following points should be noted when taking over the machine—
Check that there is a full supply of oil in the various units.

Carefully check that the oil tank, primary-chain case and gearbox levels are correct (*see* Chapter 3), that the battery is in a charged condition, "topped up" to the correct level, and that the battery connexions are secure (*see* Chapter 4). Check the tyres with a pressure gauge and adjust pressures as necessary (*see* page 77).

THE CONTROLS

Controls and Instruments. *Clutch Lever.* This is situated on the left of the handlebars. It should not be operated when the machine is in motion except to change gear and when stopping.

Front Brake Lever. This is situated on the right of the handlebars. Only gentle pressure should be applied, and the front brake should be used in conjunction with the rear brake. Handlebar adjustment is provided.

Throttle Control. A twist-grip operated by the right hand controls the throttle. Twist towards you to open and away from you to close.

Magneto Control Lever. On the left-hand side of the handlebars on 1956–59 TR5, TR6, T100, T110 and T120 models; to advance the spark close the lever anti-clockwise; to retard open the lever clockwise.

Carburettor Air Control. A lever is provided on the right-hand side of the handlebars on most 650 c.c. Triumph Twins fitted with an Amal carburettor; pull it *clockwise* to open the air valve, and close the lever to the stop provided, when it is necessary to enrich the fuel mixture for starting a *cold* engine, excluding model T120.

Where a handlebar air-control lever is not provided on 650 c.c. models having an Amal carburettor, there is a knob on top of the instrument; to close the air valve for starting a *cold* engine, press this knob down and turn it until locked.

An S.U. M.C.2 carburettor is fitted to the 1956–58 650 c.c. model 6T. With this instrument a mixture-control lever is fitted to its base and connects to the jet; raise this lever to enrich the fuel mixture for cold starting, and depress it to its lowest point for normal running afterwards (*see* page 7).

On 350 and 500 c.c. models not provided with either of the first two above-mentioned air controls, the Amal carburettor has a metal handle; prior to starting a *cold* engine, press down the handle and turn it until locked in the rich mixture position.

Horn Button. On the left of the handlebars; push to operate.

Headlamp Dipper Switch. On the left of the handlebars (combined with the horn-push on later models); depress or raise the lever to operate.

Ignition Cut-out Button. A cut-out button for stopping the engine is included on certain 500 and 650 c.c. models. In the case of models TR5, TR6 and T120 it is mounted on the near side of the handlebars, but on models T100A and T110 it is positioned in the centre of the nacelle as shown in Fig. 1. To stop the engine, depress the button. Afterwards on

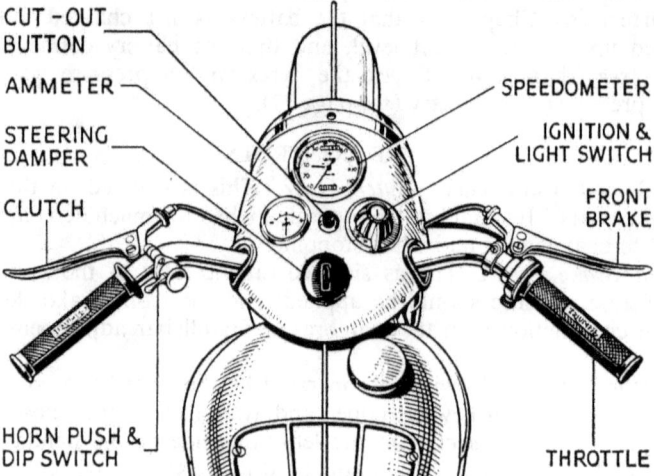

Fig. 1. Layout of Triumph handlebar controls
(Except unit construction models)

An air lever (not shown) is provided as illustrated in Fig. 2 unless the carburettor air-control is mounted on the instrument itself (see page 1). The ignition cut-out button on models T100A and T110 is fitted as shown, but on models TR5, TR6 and T120 is positioned on the near side of the handlebars. A magneto advance-and-retard control lever is near to the clutch lever on 1956–9 models TR5, TR6, T100, T110 and T120

all models having a combined lighting and coil ignition system, turn off the ignition with the key provided. This prevents battery discharge and switches off a red warning light.

Speedometer. The speedometer registers speed, trip and total mileage. Where a combined speedometer and revolution counter is fitted, the

HANDLING A TRIUMPH

central figures indicate in hundreds the engine revolutions in second, third and top gears. Speedometer illumination for night riding is controlled by the main lighting switch. To return the trip position to zero, pull down the flexible cable beneath, or on the right-hand side of, the nacelle and turn the knob *clockwise*. Do not pull the cable hard.

Lighting Switch (Dynamo Lighting). On 1956–9 models TR5, TR6, T100 and T110, and the 1959 model T120, with magneto ignition and Lucas dynamo lighting, turn the lever to operate. Switch positions—

"OFF" . . . . All lights off
"L" . . . . Tail and parking light on
"H" . . . . Tail and headlight on

On early models TR5 and TR6 the lighting switch is fitted into the headlamp, but the switch positions are the same. On the later models TR5,

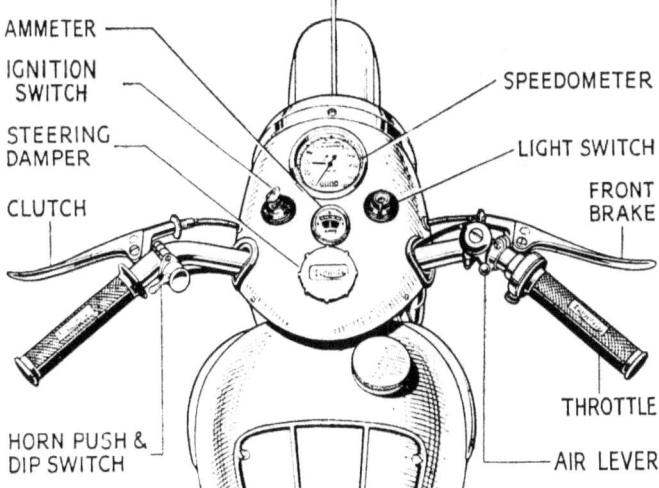

Fig. 2. Layout of Triumph handlebar controls on 1958–67 unit construction models. For 1968–9 layout see Fig. 71

The above layout applies specifically to models 3TA, 5TA and 6T, but in general is applicable to all 1958–69 unit-construction models. On some 500 and 650 c.c. models, however, an ignition cut-out button is fitted to the left side of the handlebars. All models have a key-operated ignition switch. Note that the lighting and ignition switches on models T90, T100S/S, T120 and TR6 are both mounted on the near-side panel below the dualseat; a nacelle is then omitted

TR6 and T120 the lighting switch is on the frame beneath the nose of the dualseat. On models T100 and T110 the lighting switch is located on the central nacelle.

Lighting and Ignition Switches—(a.c./d.c. Lighting-ignition Systems). On all except the five previously-mentioned 1956–9 models with magneto ignition and Lucas dynamo lighting, a combined Lucas lighting and coil-ignition system, with its battery fed from an alternator, is used. The models concerned are numerous.

Lighting Switch—Where the ignition and lighting switches are *combined* (as shown in Fig. 1), turn the switch lever as required to operate the lights. The three switch positions are—

"O" . . . . All lights off
"P" . . . . Tail and parking light on
"H" . . . . Tail and headlight on

Ignition Switch (Key)—

"Central" . . . Ignition off
"IGN" . . . . Ignition on (normal)
"EMG"* . . . Ignition on (emergency)

Where the ignition and lighting switches are *separate* (as shown in Fig. 2), the correct procedure for switch operation is—
Lighting Switch—
Turn the knob clockwise *one notch* for illuminating the tail and parking lights, and to the *second notch* for illuminating the tail lamp and headlamp main bulb. 1968–9 models have a toggle-type switch on the headlamp.
Ignition Switch—
Turn the key *clockwise* to switch on the ignition and *anti-clockwise* to switch off. In an emergency, such as a discharged battery, press in the ignition key and then turn it *anti-clockwise;* start up the power unit and afterwards turn the key *clockwise* to its normal position for engine tickover. *See* also page 7.

Ammeter. This instrument indicates the charging rate of the dynamo or alternator when the engine is running and the amount of discharge when the engine is stopped and the lights are on.

Steering Damper. To increase damping, turn the damper knob clockwise.

Oil-pressure Indicator. This button operates through the oil-pressure release valve positioned in the timing cover. The indicator button is located at the front of all 350, 500 and 650 c.c. engines on the off side, except on 350 and 500 c.c. engines from engine No. H 40528.

Where an oil-pressure indicator is fitted its button should on all 1956–69 engines not protrude until after the engine is started from *cold*, but about $\frac{1}{4}$ in. when the engine is hot and the motor-cycle travelling at about 30 m.p.h. in top gear. At about this road speed protrusion of the button should *always* begin. Only when the engine is ticking-over with the oil hot is it likely and normal for no protrusion to occur. *See* also page 26.

Foot Controls. Rear Brake. This is a flat pedal in front of the left footrest; depress to operate. Apply gently at first and increase pressure as the road speed decreases. Always use the rear brake pedal *in conjunction with* the front brake lever. On most models the pedal position is

---

* See page 7 before using this switch position and also page 48.

HANDLING A TRIUMPH

adjustable to suit that of the footrest. A knurled hand nut on the end of the brake-operating rod enables free movement of the pedal to be varied as required.

Gear Change. A small lever in front of the right-hand footrest. Move down to select a low gear and up to select a higher gear. The gear selected is shown by a small pointer on many gearboxes. Neutral position is between first and second gears, and the marking "N" on the indicator (where fitted) shows the selected position. The gear-change lever is spring loaded and always returns to the same central position. On all 1956–69 models it is fitted to a serrated shaft and can be repositioned to suit individual taste.

Kickstarter. Located behind the right-hand footrest. Earlier models TR5 and TR6 and all 1958–69 unit-construction models have the folding-pedal type.

POSITION OF CONTROLS, ETC.

It is important after buying a new or second-hand Triumph Twin to make quite sure that the position of the footrests, handlebars and all controls is such as to suit your own physical specification and provide maximum comfort and minimum difficulty while riding.

The Dualseat. Its height has been calculated to suit the physique of the average motor-cyclist, and it is not adjustable.

Footrests. On most 500 c.c. and all 650 c.c. models the offside and nearside footrests are located by two and four pegs respectively and no adjustment for position is provided. In the case of the 500 c.c. models 5TA, T100A and T100S/S, however, and on 350 c.c. models, each footrest is mounted on a taper and secured by a nut. If an adjustment for position is required, loosen the securing nut, tap the footrest until free on the taper, re-position it and then firmly re-tighten the securing nut.

Note that when the footrest positions have been altered it is often necessary to make a corresponding adjustment of the foot gear-change lever and rear brake pedal positions.

The Gear-Change Lever. On all models this is fitted to a serrated shaft and it can be re-positioned to suit individual taste; to do this loosen the set-screw and withdraw the lever from the shaft serrations. Then re-position it and firmly secure the lever by means of the set-screw.

Rear Brake Pedal. On all except some recent models the best "OFF" position of the rear brake pedal can be adjusted to suit the position of the footrest; where a near-side rear panel is provided, remove this and after slackening the brake-rod knurled adjuster nut, loosen the lock-nut on the adjustable stop-screw for the pedal and screw the latter in or out as required.

The Handlebars. You can turn these to the desired position after loosening the four "U"-bolt securing nuts, except in the case of a few 650 c.c. machines (e.g. models TR6 and T120) where the handlebars are clipped to the top lug by means of four set-screws which must first be released. After obtaining the optimum handlebar position, see that the four nuts or set-screws are *firmly* re-tightened and adjust the control lever positions if necessary.

Handlebar Control Levers. Quick accessibility and easy hand operation are essential. The position of most control levers can be adjusted to suit your personal preference after loosening the lever assembly-unit clamping screws.

STARTING

Starting the Engine from Cold (Amal Carburettor). For machines including models 3TA and 5TA, proceed as follows—

Place the gear lever in neutral (between first and second gear).

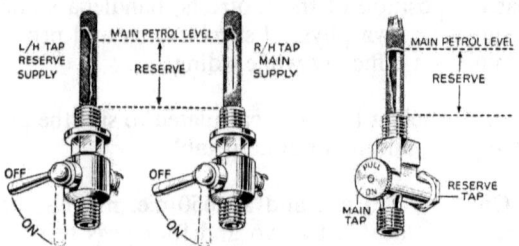

Fig. 3. The two types of petrol taps fitted

Either a pair of separate (L.H. and R.H.) lever-type taps is fitted, as shown above on the left, or else one single combined plunger-type tap is fitted as shown on the right. In both cases (except on the 1959–62 model T120) provision is made for turning on the main or reserve petrol supply. On all models turn on reserve tap (by pulling its lever down, or its hexagon-headed plunger out) only in an emergency, and when doing this do not close the main tap. When parking your mount turn off both taps

Turn the main petrol tap on.

Lift the clutch lever and operate the kickstarter two or three times. This separates the clutch plates.

In cold weather close completely the carburettor air valve (the choke) by means of the air lever on the handlebars, or the knob or wire handle on top of the Amal carburettor (*see* page 1).

Retard the spark a little by turning the control lever on 1956–59 magneto ignition models clockwise, i.e. away from the closed position.

Flood the carburettor by means of the tickler on the float bowl until the base of the carburettor is *just* wet. Over-flooding may cause difficult starting.

Turn the engine over until compression is felt on one cylinder. Free the clutch to re-position the kickstarter almost to the horizontal position.

HANDLING A TRIUMPH

Where the ignition and lighting switches are combined as shown in Fig. 1, switch on the ignition by turning the detachable ignition key to the "IGN" position. Where the ignition and lighting switches are separate as shown in Fig. 2, insert the key in the ignition switch and switch on the ignition by turning the key *clockwise*. Note that on the earlier model T100A (with independent energy-transfer ignition) no ignition switch is fitted.

Turn the twist-grip about one-eighth of a turn to open the throttle slightly. Depress the kickstarter smartly and the engine should fire immediately. Incorrectly set controls may neccessitate a second or third kick.

A model with combined lighting and ignition switch (*see* Fig. 1) may refuse to start if the battery is flat (*see* page 48). In this event turn the ignition key to "EMG"—the emergency start position. The engine will fire when the kickstarter is depressed, but as soon as the engine is running the ignition key *must* be returned to the "IGN" position.

As the engine warms up, the air lever (or air control) should be fully opened as soon as possible, otherwise the mixture strength may be too rich, in which case the oil on the cylinder walls is washed off, with harmful results. Fully advance the ignition lever on 1956-59 magneto-ignition models.

Do not allow the engine to idle slowly when cold. To warm the oil quickly and ensure proper circulation, the throttle should be adjusted to give a moderately fast tick-over.

Watch the oil-pressure indicator (where fitted) as soon as the engine starts, and remember that the indicator button *must* protrude from the release valve cap. Stop the engine and investigate the failure if the button does not protrude, or oil is not observed returning to the oil tank.

Starting from Cold (S.U. Carburettor). For the 1956-58 650 c.c. model 6T fitted with an S.U. carburettor, proceed as follows—

Engage neutral gear (N).

Turn on the main petrol tap.

With the clutch lifted, depress the kickstarter two or three times to separate the clutch plates.

To increase the strength of the mixture for a cold start, raise the jet lever on the left-hand side of the carburettor. No definite position can be given, but the rider will quickly find the best lever position. When the engine is warm, put the lever in the lowest position.

Turn the engine over by the kickstarter until compression is felt on one cylinder. By freeing the clutch, re-position the kickstarter pedal almost to the horizontal position.

Turn the key in the centre of the lighting switch to "IGN," open the throttle about one-eighth of a turn, then smartly depress the kickstarter. The engine should fire at once. If not, re-position the jet lever and the throttle. If the engine fails to start after re-setting the controls, the cause may be a flat battery. In this case turn the ignition key to the emergency start position—"EMG." The engine will then fire when the kickstarter is depressed. Return the key to the "IGN" position as soon as the engine is running.

Close the twist-grip afterwards to a moderately fast tick-over. The jet lever should be raised just enough to keep the engine running fast and evenly until it is warm and will run with the lever fully depressed.

When parking always turn the petrol tap(s) off.

RUNNING-IN

Essential. The life of your Triumph is reduced considerably if it is handled carelessly during the initial stages of running; hence some space is devoted to a discussion of the subject. To allow the bearing surfaces to harden and bed down, running-in should be carried out progressively. When intelligently and carefully handled, a machine will be faster, mechanically quieter, and will wear longer than the mount of a rider who pays no attention to the finer points which should be considered in running-in.

Throughout the 1,500 mile running-in period make full use of the excellent Triumph four-speed gearbox and change gear frequently so as to ensure that the engine never pulls too hard in a high gear, nor rotates at an excessive speed in a low gear. As the mileage increases, *progressively* increase the load, and the duration of the load, imposed on the engine and transmission. The load is, of course, mainly determined by the throttle opening, and the use of excessive throttle openings during running-in must be strictly avoided. The actual road speed attained is of lesser importance.

A new or reconditioned Triumph Twin can safely be ridden at about 50 m.p.h. on a level road if the throttle is only *slightly* opened, but this speed can be a potential cause of serious engine damage if the circumstances are such that a large throttle opening (even in a lower gear) is used over a substantial period. The use of a fairly large throttle opening, although not advised during the initial stages of running-in, is not likely to cause damage if used only momentarily.

To obtain maximum engine performance at the end of the 1,500 mile running-in period and reduce wear of moving parts to the minimum, go very easy on the throttle twist-grip, especially during the first 500 miles. *As the mileage increases, progressively increase the throttle openings used,* but strictly limit all bursts of speed, especially as regards their duration. When hill climbing, keep the throttle opening well down by intelligent use of the gearbox. This will prevent the risk of any detrimental overheating occurring.

The proper running-in of a 350, 500 or 650 c.c. Triumph engine requires the use of considerable patience and common sense rather than imposing strict limitations on road speed and throttle openings. However, during the first 250 miles it is advisable to limit the maximum throttle opening to about *one-quarter full throttle;* during the second 250 miles a maximum

HANDLING A TRIUMPH

throttle opening of about *one-third full throttle* is recommended. After covering about 500 miles gradually step up the throttle openings, but do not run on full throttle until your speedometer mileage indicator registers 1,500 miles.

When extracting the maximum power output from your Triumph engine it is advisable occasionally and momentarily to snap shut the throttle twist-grip to enable more oil to be sucked up between its cylinders and hard working pistons.

Check the various nuts for tightness after 100 miles and again at 500 miles. Also change the engine and gearbox oil (*see* pages 29 and 35). Check plugs for cleanliness every 500 miles, and the steering head for play after covering 500 miles (*see* page 70).

DON'T RUN INTO TROUBLE!

"*Live and Let Live*" should be the motto for every sensible rider handling a speedy Triumph Twin, and the author concludes this chapter by urging *you* to note and observe the following—

1 If you have a "provisional" (six month) or a "qualified" (three year) driving licence, for your own safety and the safety of others, peruse thoroughly and memorize the entire contents of *The Highway Code* published by H.M. Stationery Office and obtainable from most booksellers.

2 If you own a second-hand or a new Triumph Twin, see that it is *always* kept in a safe and legally roadworthy condition, paying special attention to the tyres, brakes, steering, lights, horn and speedometer. The last-mentioned must indicate within $\pm$ 10 per cent accuracy when 30 m.p.h. is being exceeded and, like the rear number plate, it must be easily readable by night as well as by day.

3 *Ministry of Transport Test Certificate.* A MoT certificate for road worthiness must be obtained from an authorized garage, dealer, or repair shop in respect of any motor-cycle used in the U.K. and first registered more than 3 years ago. It must be renewed *annually* and *produced* when applying for a registration licence in respect of change of ownership or renewal (Forms VE 1/2 and VE 1/A respectively), together with a current "certificate of insurance," and the registration book.

The MoT certificate costs 87p; it is legal to ride an untaxed motor-cycle to a suitable testing station after making an appointment. A certificate is issued on the spot if the motor-cycle concerned passes the required test concerning the efficiency of tyres, steering, brakes, lamps, horn, etc.

4 While riding *always*, for your own safety, wear an officially approved type of crash helmet.

2 Correct Carburation

THE 1956–58 Triumph 649 c.c. Thunderbird (Model 6T) engine has an S.U. M.C.2 type carburettor. On all other 1956–67 models Amal "Monobloc" carburettors are specified. All 1968–9 models have Amal "Concentric" carburettors fitted (*see* page 122).

AMAL "MONOBLOC" CARBURETTOR

The Amal "Monobloc" carburettor design includes: a horizontal float chamber made integral with the carburettor body; a float needle of moulded nylon; a top petrol feed; a needle jet with "bleed" holes giving two-way compensation; and a detachable pilot jet which can be easily cleaned.

Fig. 4 shows all the essential parts of the instrument. The float chamber (*13*) and needle (*9*) maintain a constant level of petrol in the needle jet (*14*) and the pilot jet (*19*). The selection by the makers of the appropriate jet sizes and main-bore choke ensures a proper atomizing and proportioning of the petrol and air sucked into the engine.

The air valve (*3*) is normally kept fully raised, and the throttle valve (*26*) controlled by the handlebar twist-grip controls the volume of mixture, and therefore the power. At all throttle openings a correct mixture is automatically obtained.

The "Monobloc" carburettor, like the earlier instrument, operates in four stages. When opening the throttle from the fully closed position to one-eighth open (for tick-over) the mixture is supplied by the pilot jet (*19*), and the strength of the mixture is determined by the setting of the knurled pilot air-adjusting screw (*22*) which has a coil locking spring to facilitate adjustment. As the throttle is opened slightly farther, the main jet system comes into action, the mixture being augmented by the main jet (*17*) through the pilot by-pass and air passage (*6*).

The amount of cut-away on the atmospheric side of the throttle valve regulates the petrol-to-air ratio between one-eighth and one-quarter throttle. The needle-jet (*14*) and the jet needle (*25*) take over the mixture regulation between one-quarter and three-quarter throttle, and the mixture strength is determined by the relative position of the needle in the clip (*4*) attached to the throttle valve (*26*). When the throttle is opened beyond three-quarters, the mixture strength is determined only by the size of the main jet. Note that the main jet (*17*) does not spray petrol

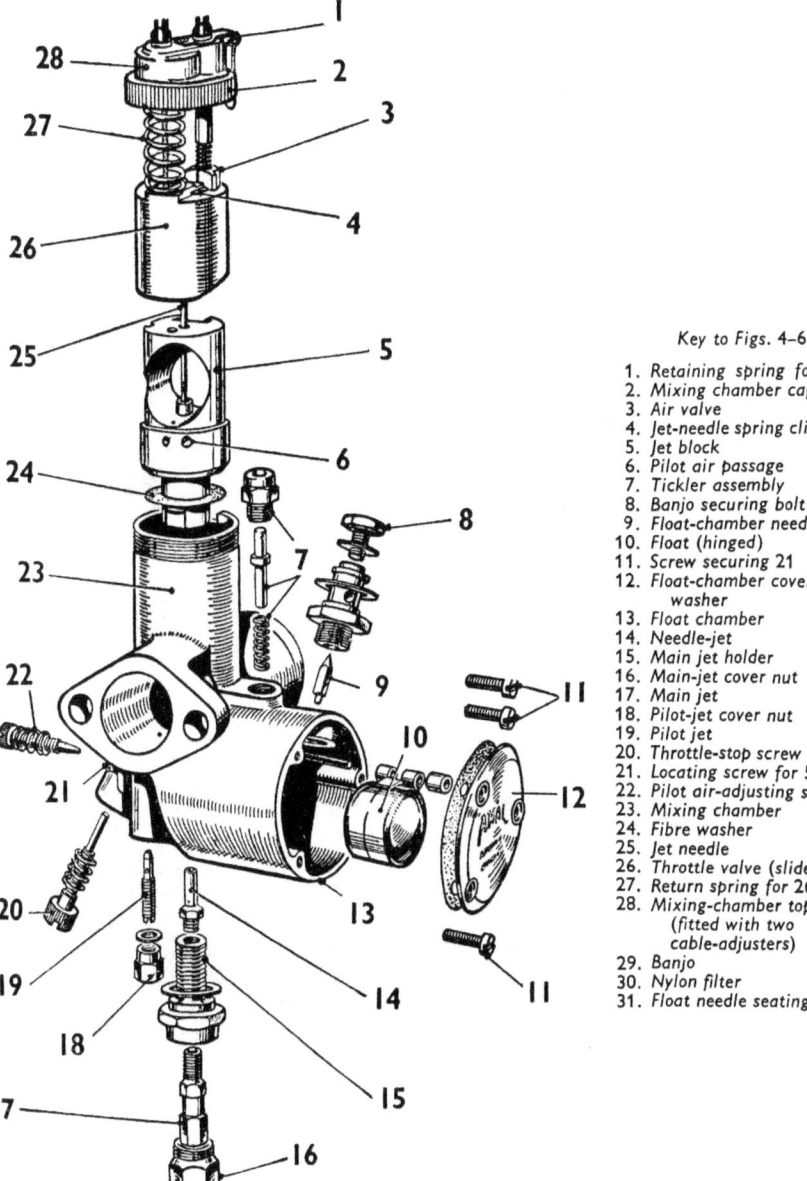

Key to Figs. 4–6
1. Retaining spring for 2
2. Mixing chamber cap ring
3. Air valve
4. Jet-needle spring clip
5. Jet block
6. Pilot air passage
7. Tickler assembly
8. Banjo securing bolt
9. Float-chamber needle
10. Float (hinged)
11. Screw securing 21
12. Float-chamber cover and washer
13. Float chamber
14. Needle-jet
15. Main jet holder
16. Main-jet cover nut
17. Main jet
18. Pilot-jet cover nut
19. Pilot jet
20. Throttle-stop screw
21. Locating screw for 5
22. Pilot air-adjusting screw
23. Mixing chamber
24. Fibre washer
25. Jet needle
26. Throttle valve (slide)
27. Return spring for 26
28. Mixing-chamber top (fitted with two cable-adjusters)
29. Banjo
30. Nylon filter
31. Float needle seating

Fig. 4. Exploded view of Amal "Monobloc" carburettor (All 1956–67 350, 500 and 650 c.c. Triumph Twins)

(By courtesy of B.S.A. Motor Cycles Ltd.)

direct into the carburettor mixing-chamber, but discharges through the needle-jet into the primary air chamber. From there it enters the main choke through the primary air choke. The latter has a two-way compensating action in conjunction with the "bleed" holes in the needle-jet. Pilot and main jet behaviour are not affected by this two-way compensation which governs only acceleration at normal cruising speed.

TUNING THE AMAL "MONOBLOC" CARBURETTOR

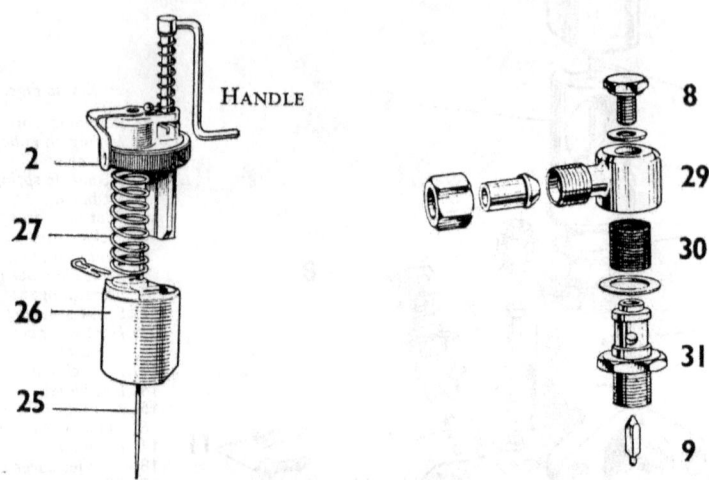

Figs. 5, 6. Showing (left) the air control handle fitted to the Amal carburettor on many 350, 500 and 650 Triumph Twins, and (right) the gauze filter incorporated in the banjo of the petrol feed pipe

Alternative types of air control provided are a handlebar lever or a knob on top of the carburettor (see page 1). On most Triumph Twins of recent design the banjo shown at (29) is integral with the petrol pipe and there is no union nut as shown in Fig. 6

Keep to the Maker's Setting. Except in abnormal circumstances it is most unwise to completely retune your Amal carburettor or to vary the setting recommended by The Triumph Engineering Co. Ltd. and given on page 14. However, it is usually necessary at some time to alter the slow-running adjustment by means of the pilot air-adjusting screw and the throttle-stop screw.

On rare occasions it may be desirable to vary the strength of the fuel mixture for general running by altering the size of the main jet, the needle position, or possibly the throttle valve cut-away, but any or all of these alterations should not be made unless *really* required to offset a serious decline in engine performance. The condition of the sparking plugs provides an excellent guide to the condition of the mixture sucked into the combustion chambers. The body of both plugs should be black with no sooty deposits.

CORRECT CARBURATION

Note the Following. Referring to Fig. 4, the throttle-stop screw (*20*) should always be kept adjusted so that the engine ticks-over nicely at a *moderate* speed (neither too fast nor too slow) when the throttle twist-grip is completely closed.

The pilot air-adjusting screw (*22*) meters the amount of air mixed with the petrol and thus controls the suction imposed on the pilot jet (*19*). Screwing it out or in weakens or enriches the mixture respectively. The normal setting to ensure good tick-over is to unscrew it about $2\frac{1}{2}$ turns.

The jet needle (*25*), having its lower end tapered, allows more or less petrol to pass through the needle-jet (*14*) according to the relative positions of the above-mentioned needle and jet. Raising and lowering the needle (attached to the throttle valve) enriches and weakens the mixture respectively, and it is therefore most important to see that the jet-needle clip (*4*) engages the correct groove below the top of the needle (i.e. the needle position). On all Triumph Twins the correct needle positions are those tabulated on page 14, but note that on some earlier models without unit construction of engine and gearbox the needle position set by the makers, and intended for the first 1,000 miles running, was the *fourth* notch from the top. In the case of an earlier model, check and if necessary make the required adjustment.

The throttle-valve cut-away influences the depression on the main fuel supply and enables tuning, where essential, to be effected between the pilot and needle-jet range of throttle opening. Note that the number marked on the throttle valve (e.g. $376/3\frac{1}{2}$) indicates a type 376 throttle valve with a No. $3\frac{1}{2}$ cut-away. Larger and smaller cut-away numbers give a weaker and richer mixture respectively. An alteration from the recommended cut-away is very seldom necessary.

Slow-running Adjustment. This should be effected with the engine already warmed up. If the adjustment is appreciably at fault, screw home the pilot air-adjusting screw fully and then unscrew it (usually about three half turns) until the engine idles at an excessive speed, with the throttle twist-grip closed and the throttle slide abutting the throttle-stop screw. The air lever should be fully open and the ignition lever (where automatic ignition-advance is not provided) should be set to obtain the best slow-running (half to two-thirds advanced).

Referring to Fig. 4, unscrew the throttle-stop screw (*20*) until the engine slows up and begins to falter. Then screw the pilot air-adjusting screw (*22*) in or out as required to enable the engine to run regularly and faster. To weaken the mixture, screw the pilot air-adjusting screw *outwards*.

Slowly lower the throttle-stop screw until the engine again commences to falter and reset the pilot air-adjusting screw to obtain the best slow-running. If after making this second adjustment the engine ticks over too fast, repeat the adjustment a third time. The combined adjustment sounds complicated but in practice is quite simple. It is important to avoid excessive richness of the slow-running mixture, especially if much riding is done on small throttle openings; if the mixture is too rich, considerable running on the pilot jet will occur while riding, with consequently a high fuel consumption. The mixture should border on the weak side, with the engine almost on the point of spitting-back.

Aim at obtaining the best even tick-over at a *moderate speed*. Too slow a tick-over is not advised because it is apt to result in insufficient

Triumph Model	Main Jet	Pilot Jet	Throttle Valve	Needle-Jet	Needle Position
350 c.c. TRIUMPH ENGINES					
3TA (1958–66)					
To Engine H 40528	110	25	375/3½	0·105	3
After the above Engine	100	25	375/3½	0·015	3
T90 (1963–67)	180	20	376/3½	0·016	3
500 c.c. TRIUMPH ENGINES					
5T (1956–58)	200	30	376/3½	0·106	3
5TA (1959–66)					
To Engine H 40528	160	25	375/3	0·105	3
After above Engine	190	25	376/3½	0·105	3
T100 (1956–9)	220	25	376/3¼	0·106	3
T100A, T100S/S (1960–67)					
To Engine H 18612	160	25	375/3	0·105	3
After above Engine	190	25	376/3½	0·106	3
650 c.c. TRIUMPH ENGINES					
6T (1958–60)*	270	25	376/3½	0·106	3
6T (1961–67)					
Engines D.7727–D.11192	220	25	376/4	0·106	3
TR5 (1956–58)	220	25	376/3½	0·106	3
TR6, TR6S/S (1956–67)					
To Engine DU 5825	250†	25	376/3½	0·106	3
After above Engine	310	25	389/3¼	0·106	1
T110 (1956–60)	250†	25	376/3½	0·106	3
T110 (1961), Nos. D.7727–D.11192	220	25	376/4	0·106	3
T120 (1956–67)					
To Engine DU 5825	240	25	376/3	0·106¼	3
After above Engine	260	25	389/3	0·106	2

* Amal monobloc type carburettors are fitted to all 1956–67 350, 500 and 650 c.c. models with the exception of the 1956–58 650 c.c. Model 6T. This machine has an S.U. type M.C.2 carburettor with a 0·090 in. main jet.

† To obtain the maximum possible performance it is advisable to withdraw the air cleaner rubber hose and fit a No. 270 main jet.

lubrication of the cylinder bores and pistons while the engine is hot. Too fast a tick-over can cause detrimental overheating as well as excessive noise.

Synchronizing Twin Carburettors. On the Bonneville 120 (model T120) the twin Amal carburettors may need to be synchronized in the following manner. Adjust the junction-box cables so that the free play of both cables is at a minimum. Start the engine and remove one sparking plug lead. Now adjust the pilot air-adjusting screw and throttle-stop screw on the other carburettor until the engine runs smoothly at a normal tick-over

CORRECT CARBURATION 15

speed. Then replace the sparking plug lead and repeat the procedure for the carburettor attached to the cylinder whose sparking plug lead has been replaced.

Having replaced both sparking plug h.t. leads and made individual carburettor slow-running adjustments for each cylinder, you will probably find that engine tick-over speed is rather excessive. If this is so, lower the two throttle-stop screws simultaneously as required. Note that it is absolutely essential that *both* throttle valves are simultaneously moved the same distance as the throttle twist-grip is turned. If this does not occur, some rough running will probably result, especially during acceleration.

Possible Causes of Poor Slow-running. In the rather unlikely event of it being found impossible to obtain or maintain good slow-running after making the combined pilot air-adjusting screw and throttle-stop screw adjustment as described on page 13, a thorough investigation should be made for the cause; it may be one or more of the following—
1 Air leaks caused by worn inlet-valve guides;
2 Badly seating valves or no clearances, causing a weak mixture;
3 Air leaks caused by a poor joint between the Amal carburettor flange(s) and the cylinder-head induction manifold, or by some distortion of the carburettor flange(s);
4 An obstructed pilot jet, or incorrect float-chamber level;
5 Excessive accumulation of carbon deposits on the piston crowns and in the combustion chambers;
6 The use of an unsuitable type of sparking plugs;
7 Running with sparking plugs which have become oily or dirty, or having an incorrect gap between their electrodes;
8 An incorrect contact-breaker gap;
9 Incorrect ignition timing;
10 Faulty insulation of the h.t. plug leads or a faulty battery.

An Obstructed Pilot Jet. The fuel passage to the pilot jet of the Amal carburettor is very narrow and can therefore easily become choked. Referring to Fig. 4, to remove the pilot jet (*19*), remove its cover nut (*18*) and then unscrew the jet itself. Clean this jet thoroughly; do not use fine wire but blow through it, using the tyre pump. It is also important to see that the air passage (*6*) to the pilot jet (*19*) is not obstructed. Blow through this air passage and also the pilot outlet.

Excessive Petrol Consumption. Occasionally the petrol consumption is excessive in spite of the carburettor or carburettors being carefully tuned for good slow-running. Possible causes are many. The most likely ones are: a poor float-chamber cover joint; a damaged float; sticking of the moulded-nylon float needle; a slack main-jet cover nut; a slack main-jet holder; a worn needle-jet; a loose pilot jet; and slackness of petrol pipe union nuts. All the foregoing are likely to cause petrol leakage. Likely causes of excessive petrol consumption through power loss are: binding of the brake shoes on the brake drums through incorrect adjustment; slipping of the clutch because of worn friction inserts or bad adjustment; and poor engine compression due to badly seating valves and/or poor piston ring fit.

Less likely possible causes of high petrol consumption are: air leaks between the carburettor flange(s) and the induction manifold; wear of the inlet-valve guides; incorrect valve clearances; weak valve springs; and late ignition timing.

A careful investigation of the cause of excessive petrol consumption should be made, but do not attempt to reduce consumption by fitting a smaller size main jet to one or both carburettors (where two are fitted). The main jet size has no effect on petrol consumption unless the throttle is more than half open. If it is difficult or impossible to diagnose the real cause of a high petrol consumption after making big efforts, try lowering the tapered jet-needle *one notch*. When doing this make quite sure that the jet-needle clip beds home securely in the needle groove.

AMAL CARBURETTOR MAINTENANCE (1956–67)

To ensure correct carburation it is advisable occasionally to remove the carburettor from the engine, strip it down completely, and then thoroughly clean and inspect the various components. It is a good plan to do this about every six months as described for single-carburettor engines.

To Remove Amal "Monobloc" Carburettor. First remove the air filter where fitted (*see* page 20). Also close the petrol taps and disconnect the petrol pipes from the tank and from the float chamber of the carburettor by unscrewing the pipe union nuts and removing the banjo securing bolt shown at (*8*) in Fig. 4. Remove both pipes and fully close the throttle twist-grip and the air control.

Referring to Fig. 4, unscrew the mixing chamber cap ring (*2*) and remove the two nuts securing the carburettor flange to the induction manifold assembly, details of which are shown in Fig. 7. Then, except on later unit-construction models (*see* page 107), remove the carburettor from its mounting studs on the manifold. While removing the carburettor withdraw the slides (throttle valve and air valve) from the mixing chamber and tie them up in a convenient position out of the way.

Closely examine the gasket, insulating block and rubber "O" ring shown in Fig. 7. If there is any damage which could adversely affect an air-tight joint, renew the item(s) concerned immediately.

Dismantling the Carburettor. Referring to Fig. 4, the required procedure is quite straightforward. First remove the jet-needle spring clip (*4*) from the top of the throttle valve slide (*26*), and the tapered jet needle (*25*) from the throttle valve. Then compress the throttle-valve return spring (*27*) until the nipple on the end of the throttle cable can be freed from the

CORRECT CARBURATION 17

slot at the base of the throttle valve and the latter withdrawn. It is also advisable to remove the air valve (*3*) from its control cable or carburettor control device (*see* Fig. 5).

Next tackle the float chamber. Remove the three slotted screws (*11*) securing the float chamber cover (*12*) to the float chamber (*13*) and withdraw the float-spindle bush and the hinged float (*10*). Afterwards remove the moulded-nylon float-chamber needle (*9*) and lay these items aside in a safe place along with other carburettor components being

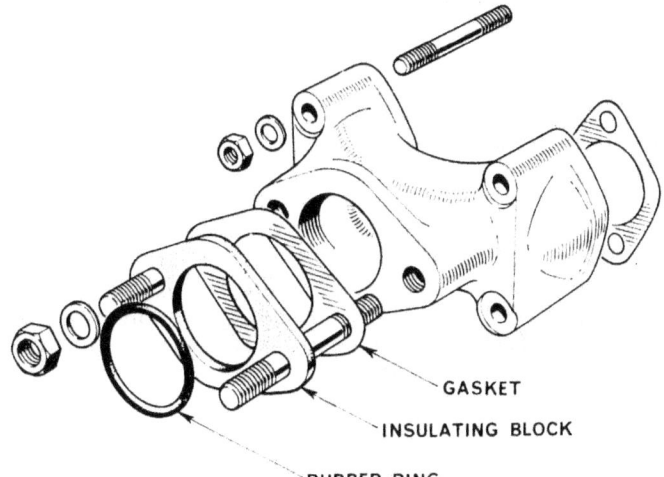

Fig. 7. Showing details of the induction manifold assembly

This does not, of course, apply to the Bonneville 120 engine with twin carburettors. In this case two separate induction manifolds are screwed into the cylinder head

(*From Triumph Workshop Manual*)

removed. Note that the float chamber vent is embodied in the tickler assembly (*7*) and also that a fine gauze filter (*30*) is included inside the banjo (*29*) for the petrol pipe as shown in Fig. 6. Remove and handle this small cylindrical filter most carefully. It should not be necessary to remove the tickler assembly, but it is desirable to remove the float-chamber needle seating (*31*) if you wish to check the efficiency of the very small float-chamber needle.

To remove the main jet (*17*), unscrew the main-jet cover nut (*16*) and then unscrew the main jet from its holder (*15*). To remove the needle-jet (*14*) from the main-jet holder (*15*), unscrew the latter and then unscrew the needle-jet itself.

Remove the jet block (*5*) in the following manner. After first unscrewing the small jet-block locating screw (*21*) replace the main-jet holder (*15*) and then tap it *gently* until the block and fibre washer (*24*) can be withdrawn from the top of the mixing chamber (*23*). To complete carburettor dismantling, remove the pilot jet (*19*); remove its cover nut (*18*) and washer and then unscrew the jet from the body of the carburettor.

Cleaning the Instrument. Wash all the carburettor components thoroughly clean with petrol and blow through the various ducts and passages to make sure that they are quite clear. Avoid using a fluffy rag for drying purposes. Pay special attention to the small pilot air passage (6) in the jet block. See that all impurities are removed from inside the float chamber. On the "Monobloc" carburettor do not forget to clean the detachable pilot jet and the filter gauze inside the top-feed union for the float chamber.

Inspecting the Parts. When dismantling the carburettor it is advisable to make a close inspection of the various parts if the carburettor has been in continuous service for a considerable period.

(1) *The Float Chamber.* Examine the components very carefully and check that the vent is unobstructed. The float must be in perfect condition. Check that it does not leak by shaking it; the movement of any petrol inside will be immediately audible. Never try and repair a damaged float, but always fit a new one. Clean the moulded-nylon float needle thoroughly and check it for efficient action by inverting the float needle seating (shown at (*31*) in Fig. 6), with needle in position, pouring a little petrol into the aperture around the needle, and checking for any leakage when pressure is applied on the needle.

Examine the joint faces of the float chamber and float-chamber cover for any bruising or damage which would prevent the joint being petrol-tight after assembly.

(2) *The Throttle Valve.* Test this for good fit and no slackness in the mixing chamber. Look for excessive scoring on the front side and excessive wear on its rear face. If close inspection reveals excessive wear, renew the slide and when doing this make quite sure that the new slide has the correct degree of cut-away (*see* page 13).

(3) *The Air Valve.* Inspect this also for excessive wear and make sure there is no slackness. Verify the proper fit of the slide in the jet block. Check that the return springs for the throttle valve and the air valve are in perfect condition and have not lost their compressive strength.

(4) *The Jet-needle Clip.* The spring clip securing the tapered needle to the throttle valve must grip the needle firmly, and free rotation must *not* occur, as this causes the needle groove to wear. Always be careful to replace the needle with the clip in the correct groove (*see* page 14).

(5) *The Needle-jet.* Look for wear and possible scoring of its orifice which usually occurs after covering about 15,000 miles. The movement of the stainless-steel jet needle is ultimately bound to cause some wear.

(6) *The Jet Block.* Before tapping this home in the mixing chamber verify by blowing that the pilot air duct is clear and that the jet-block fibre seal is in good condition.

(7) *The Carburettor Flange.* Examine this for truth with a straight-edge.

CORRECT CARBURATION 19

Distortion sometimes occurs, and this may cause an air leak. If the flange face is slightly concave, file and rub down the face with emery cloth laid on a surface plate until it is dead flat and smooth. Alternatively have it faced on a machine. Renew the rubber "O" ring (*see* Fig. 7) unless perfect and see that the heat-resisting washer is in sound condition.

(8) *The Petrol Filter.* Check that the cylindrical gauze filter shown at (30) in Fig. 6 is quite serviceable and that the gauze itself has not anywhere separated from its supporting structure. If the filter is not perfect, renew it immediately.

Wear of Jet Needle. The needle itself does *not* wear, though some wear of the groove may occur if the jet-needle clip is not grasping the needle firmly. If the mixture is too rich with the clip in No. 1 groove (nearest top end), it is probable that the needle-jet needs to be renewed because of wear. It is assumed that the carburettor is correctly tuned and that no flooding occurs.

Assembling "Monobloc" Carburettor. Do this in the reverse order of dismantling. Referring to Fig. 4, screw home the pilot jet (*19*) and the pilot-jet cover nut (*18*); remember to replace its washer. Push or tap home the jet block (*5*) and fibre seal (*24*) through the large end of the mixing chamber (*23*). Check that the fibre seal fitted to the stub of the jet block is in good condition. Then fit the jet-block locating-screw (*21*). Screw the main-jet holder (*15*) into the jet block, after checking that the washer for the holder is sound, and that the needle-jet (*14*) is screwed firmly into the top of the main-jet holder. Replace the main jet (*17*) and its cover-nut (*16*).

Replace the moulded-nylon needle (*9*) in the float chamber (*13*), and fit the hinged float (*10*) with the *narrow* side of the hinge uppermost. Afterwards fit the float-chamber cover (*12*) and secure by means of the three screws (*11*). Verify that the cover and body faces are undamaged and quite clean. Renew the washer.

If previously removed, attach the jet needle (*25*) to the throttle valve (*26*) and secure with the jet-needle clip (*4*), making sure that the clip enters the correct groove.

Replace the tickler assembly (*7*) if this has previously been removed, and fit all items shown in Fig. 6, leaving the banjo bolt (*8*) for final tightening down later. Note that the small cylindrical gauze filter (*30*) has longitudinal supports moulded to its sides. When replacing this filter see that these supports do not obstruct the feed holes in the float-needle seating (*31*), otherwise some petrol starvation may result.

To Replace Amal Carburettor. With the gasket, insulating block and rubber "O" ring correctly located (*see* Fig. 7) on the face of the induction manifold, position the carburettor flange over the manifold studs after first re-connecting the throttle valve and air valve to their respective cables, smearing a little oil over the slides and then easing the latter gently down into the mixing chamber. When easing the throttle valve home, make sure that the tapered jet needle (25) really enters the hole in the jet block (5). Secure the carburettor flange firmly to the manifold by means of the two nuts, and tighten these evenly. Tighten down firmly the mixing-chamber knurled cap-ring (2) and see that the throttle slide works freely when this is tightened down.

Finally reconnect the petrol pipe(s) and firmly retighten the petrol pipe union nuts and the banjo bolt shown at (8) in Fig. 6. Replace the air filter where provided, and replacement is now complete.

THE AIR FILTER (1956–69)

Removing the Filter from Carburettor. On earlier Triumphs not of the unit-construction type and having the "D"-shaped type filter shown in Fig. 8, servicing the filter, except on some models (e.g. models 6T and T110), necessitates the removal of the oil tank after draining it, disconnecting the oil pipes, and removing the three tank securing bolts. After disconnecting the rubber sleeve shown at (6) and (7) in Fig. 8 the air filter can then be removed. Where oil tank removal on earlier models with separate gearboxes is not necessary the filter assembly can be easily removed after detaching the rear panels or (on many later models) the battery and battery carrier. In the latter case the filter can be lifted clear of the bottom spigot after removing its top bolt.

On all 650 c.c. models with unit-construction of the engine and gearbox, which have a single carburettor, and are fitted with the "O"-shaped type filter shown in Fig. 10, removal of the filter necessitates preliminary removal of the off-side panel (where fitted) from the machine as follows; unscrew the two front panel junction screws, the two domed nuts, and a nut just beneath the rear of the petrol tank. Also on a Trophy model TR6 remove the switch panel. After loosening the central circular clip then slide the air filter off the carburettor adaptor. If any difficulty is experienced, dismantle the air filter *in situ*. Two filters are provided on twin-carburettor models.

On all 350 and 500 c.c. models with unit-construction of the engine and gearbox and fitted with the "O"-shaped type air filter shown in Fig. 10, removal of the filter only entails slackening the central circular clip and then withdrawing the air filter from the carburettor adaptor. As in the case of the 650 c.c. unit-construction models, if difficulty is experienced in removing the complete filter, dismantle it in position on the carburettor.

Dismantling and Assembling the Filter. If it is of the "D" type shown in Fig. 8, unscrew the cover screw (3), remove the cover and then extract the filter element. Should it be of the "O" type shown in Fig. 10, remove the screwed clip securing the outer perforated case, next the back plate, then the filter element, and afterwards slide the front plate from over the carburettor adaptor.

Assemble the air filter in the reverse order of dismantling. After

CORRECT CARBURATION

reassembling a "D"-shaped type filter see that the cover screw is firmly tightened, and after assembling an "O"-shaped type filter make sure that the perforated-case clip, and the circular clip securing the air filter assembly to the carburettor are both tightened firmly.

Servicing the Filter Element. This is recommended about every 3,000 miles. Having removed the "dry" fabric element from a "D"-shaped air filter, wash the element thoroughly with petrol until all road dust is eliminated. Then allow the element to dry off and re-oil it with "Vokes Trifiltrine" filter oil or grade SAE.20 engine oil. Change the filter element about every 10,000 miles. A choked filter causes loss of power and high petrol consumption.

After removing a "dry" filter element (felt) from an "O"-shaped filter (*see* Fig. 9) rinse the element in clean paraffin or kerosene and allow it to drain thoroughly before assembling the filter. *On no account oil a felt-type filter.*

Some "Bonneville" T120 models with twin carburettors have a single large air filter incorporating a *paper* element. This element should be dismantled and blown clear or renewed as required. It should not be washed or oiled.

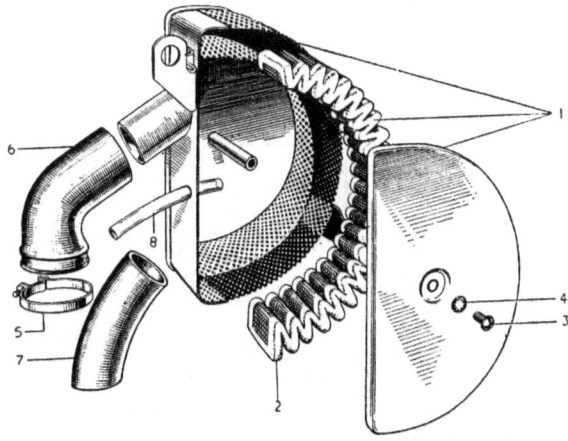

Fig. 8. "D"-shaped type air filter ("wet" element)
(*Triumph Engineering Co. Ltd.*)

This type of air filter is fitted to the carburettors of many 1956–62 pre-unit construction Triumph twins; most 1958–69 unit-construction models have the more attractive and modern filter shown in Fig. 10 fitted as standard equipment.

1. Filter assembly
2. Filter element (C and A)
3. Cover screw
4. Shakeproof washer
5. Clip connexion to carburettor
6. Connexion, Amal carburettor to filter (rubber)
7. Connexion, S.U. carburettor to filter (rubber)
8. Vent pipe, carburettor to filter

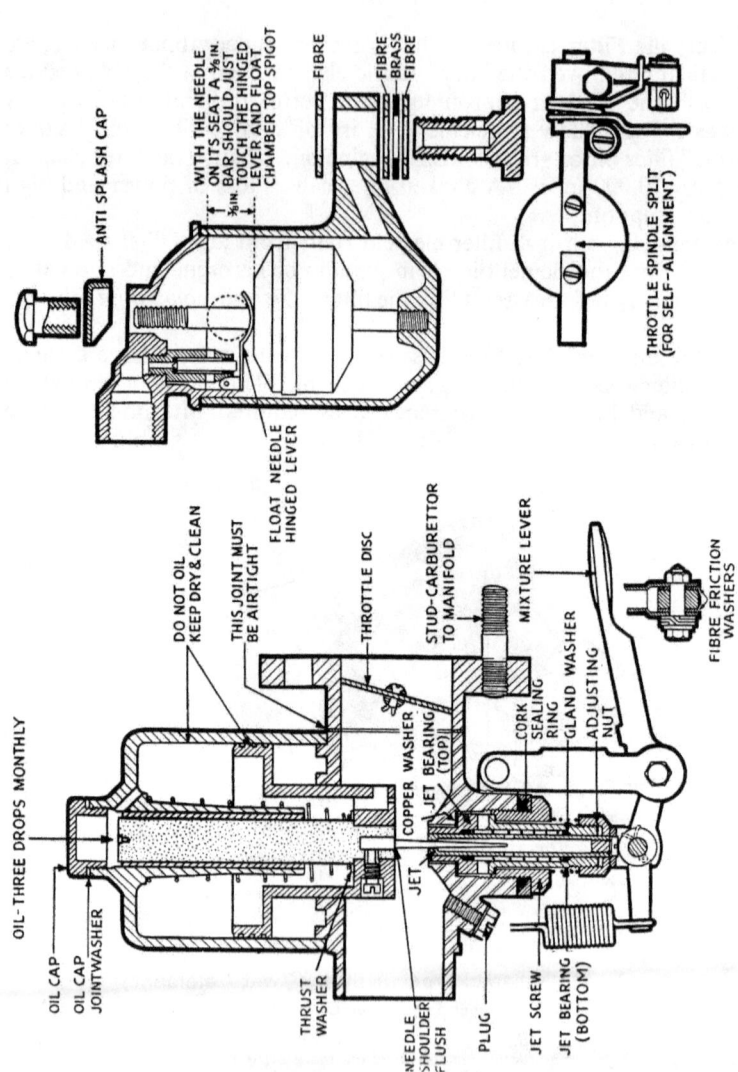

Fig. 9. Sectioned arrangement of S.U. M.C.2 carburettor

CORRECT CARBURATION 23

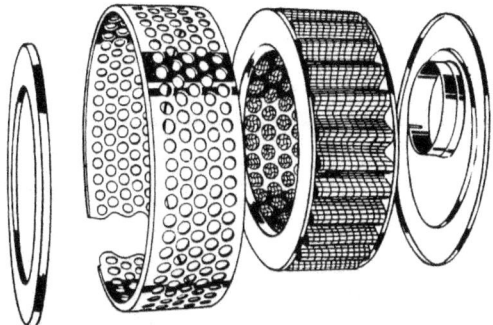

Fig. 10. "O"-shaped type air filter ("dry" C and A element)
(From Triumph Workshop Manual)

THE S.U. M.C.2. CARBURETTOR (1956-8)

The S.U. carburettor is of the automatically expanding type in which the cross-sectional area of the air passage and the effective orifice of the jet is variable.

Adjustment and Tuning. It is not advisable that the needle type which governs the effective orifice of the jet should be changed from the maker's original specification, as this is determined for a particular engine after considerable testing, both on the engine test bed and on road test with premium grade petrols. Low grade and alcohol-blended fuels may require the fitting of a richer than standard needle.

If in doubt regarding the correctness of the type fitted, check by removing the suction chamber, then by slackening the needle side screw when the needle can be removed and its markings by numbers or letters noted. These identifying markings may be rolled round the shank, or stamped on the flat end. Only this needle should be changed to alter the mixture strength, as all jets are of standard size and the jet adjusting nut is for setting the idling only. It is essential that the needle be fitted with its shoulder flush with the face of the piston, as shown in Fig. 9.

When detaching the suction chamber and piston assembly from the main carburettor body to check or change the needle, remove the oil cap and the two side screws and lift the assembly off the carburettor body.

Tuning the carburettor is confined to correct idling adjustment by means of the throttle-stop screw, which governs the amount of throttle opening for idling speed, and the jet adjusting nut (Fig. 9) which controls the idling mixture. Screwing this nut up weakens the mixture, screwing it down enriches it. This nut must not be forced, as this may set the jet off centre.

A too rich idling mixture gives a rhythmical or regular misfire with a trace of black in the exhaust. A too weak mixture gives an irregular type of misfire with a tendency to stop. A correct mixture gives an even beat with a colourless exhaust.

3 Triumph Lubrication

THE oil film between the various contacting surfaces of the working parts of a motor-cycle is equal in importance to the quality of the materials used in making the various components of the machine. Adequate and proper lubrication means supplying a sufficient quantity of the right kind of oil or grease. If the quantity of lubricant is sufficient but the quality is low and the grade incorrect or, on the other hand, if the quality and grade are correct but the supply deficient, trouble is certain to be encountered and the serviceable life of the motor-cycle reduced.

ENGINE LUBRICATION

The engine operates at a high speed and this is conducive to comparatively high temperatures, so it is imperative that only oils of the best and proved quality be used. Lubricant in constant circulation collects many substances, such as unburnt fuel, moisture through condensation, carbon, and gritty and metallic particles of an abrasive nature; these all create wear and should be extracted without delay. The selection of the oil is in the hands of the motor-cyclist, and it is also his duty to look after the system. Recommended lubricants are listed on page 26.

The Triumph Dry Sump System. A dry-sump lubrication system is employed on all 1956–69 Triumph models. The oil is gravity-fed from the oil tank through a filter and pipe to the pressure side of the oil pump. The pump (*see* Fig. 11) is a double-plunger type, fitted with two non-return valves. The oil is forced through drilled passage-ways to the crankshaft, and from the big-ends the oil issues as a fog to lubricate the pistons and other internal engine parts. *See* also Fig. 56.

The oil pressure between the oil pump and the crankshaft is controlled by an oil-pressure release valve. This valve is situated in the timing cover, or on all later unit-construction models adjacent to the timing cover at the front of the crankcase on the off side.

On all 650 c.c. models and all 350 and 500 c.c. models up to 1965 engine No. H 40528 the oil-pressure release valve (*see* Fig. 12) consists of a piston, main spring, secondary spring, oil seal and button indicator. The valve is forced back on the auxiliary spring when the engine is running, this being shown by the button protruding through the valve cap. The piston is moved still farther back on the main spring when the oil pressure is

TRIUMPH LUBRICATION

excessive, thus allowing oil to be by-passed through the release-valve body to the crankcase where it is scavenged to the oil tank.

On all 1965-69 350 and 500 c.c. unit-construction models from engine No. H 40528 onwards the oil-pressure release valve (*see* Fig. 13) does not include a button indicator and oil pressure is automatically controlled by a single spring.

After passing through the engine, oil falls to the bottom of the crankcase where it is filtered. The crankcase oil return pipe (visible as it protrudes through the filter when the sump plate is removed) then returns the oil to the suction side of the oil pump to be returned to the oil tank. The suction oil-pump plunger has double the capacity of the pressure side; this ensures that no liquid oil remains on the floor of the crankcase. The valve rockers are lubricated by oil taken from the return scavenge pipe by tapping the supply just below the oil tank. After being forced through the rocker spindles, into the rocker boxes and through the rocker arms, the oil lubricates the valve stems and push-rod cups. The oil drains from the

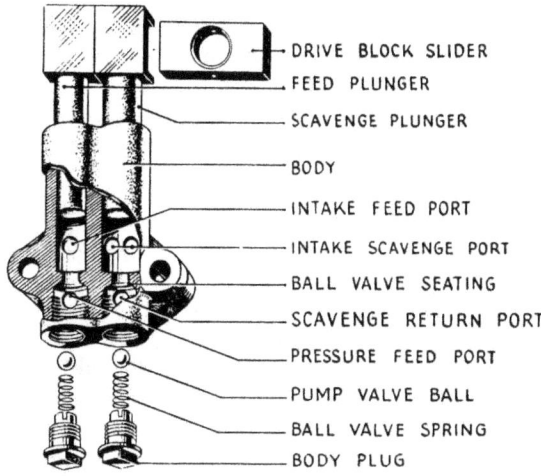

Fig. 11. Oil pump (1956 onwards)

valve wells in the cylinder head into the push-rod cover tubes, where it lubricates the tappets and finally drains into the sump.

Forget the Pump. The dry sump lubrication is so simple that it functions for a long time without attention to the actual pumping mechanism. It will readily be realized, however, that the duties of changing the oil and cleaning the filters must be carried out at regular intervals.

Five Essential Lubrication Points. In order to obtain maximum performance and long life from your Triumph Twin engine, always remember and *observe* the following five essential points—

1 Always keep the oil tank topped-up to the correct level with suitable engine oil of the correct grade.
2 To ensure proper lubrication of the crankshaft, cylinder bores, pistons, and engine bearings, always run-in a new or rebored engine with the utmost care during the first 1,500 miles.
3 Regularly check that the engine oil is circulating properly.
4 Keep the engine oil clean by changing the oil in the tank at regular intervals.
5 Clean the filters in the oil tank and sump regularly.

Suitable Engine Oils. Never run on a good brand of engine oil of unsuitable grade, or on an inferior brand. After exhaustive tests the Triumph Engineering Co. Ltd. recommend for all engines the use (in the U.K.) of one of the following six oils—
1 Castrol XL (summer) or Castrolite (winter).
2 Mobiloil A (summer) or Arctic (winter).
3 Shell X-100 30 (summer) or X-100 20W (winter).
4 B.P. Energol SAE.30 (summer) or SAE.20W (winter).
5 Esso Extra Motor Oil 20W/30 (summer and winter).
6 Regent Havoline SAE.30 (summer) or SAE.20W (winter).

Running-in Procedure. For sound advice on how to run-in a new or rebored Triumph Twin engine, *see* page 8.

Topping-up the Oil Tank. About every 250 miles check the level of oil in the tank and if necessary top-up the tank with one of the six engine oils previously recommended. On many 350 and 500 c.c. unit-construction Triumphs (e.g. models 3TA and 5TA) to obtain access to the tank filler cap it is necessary to raise the dualseat (*see* Fig. 55). On other models the filler cap is readily accessible on the off side of the oil tank.

On all Triumph Twins the oil tank is correctly topped-up when the oil level is 1½ in. (4 cm) below the filler cap. Further topping-up should be avoided as this causes excessive venting through the oil tank breather pipe because of lack of air space. To prevent excessive topping-up it is desirable always to run the engine for a few minutes prior to pouring in the oil. After the engine is left stationary for a considerable time an appreciable quantity of engine oil drains into the sump and is not returned to the oil tank by the scavenge side of the oil pump. Too low an oil level, on the other hand, can cause overheating of the engine because of an insufficient volume of oil in circulation. *See* also page 121.

Check Oil Circulation Regularly. On all 650 c.c. engines and all 350 and 500 c.c. engines up to engine No. H 40528 the oil pressure and circulation can be checked regularly by means of the button protruding from the oil-pressure release valve shown in Fig. 14. When the engine is stationary the button on the end of the indicator shaft should be flush with the

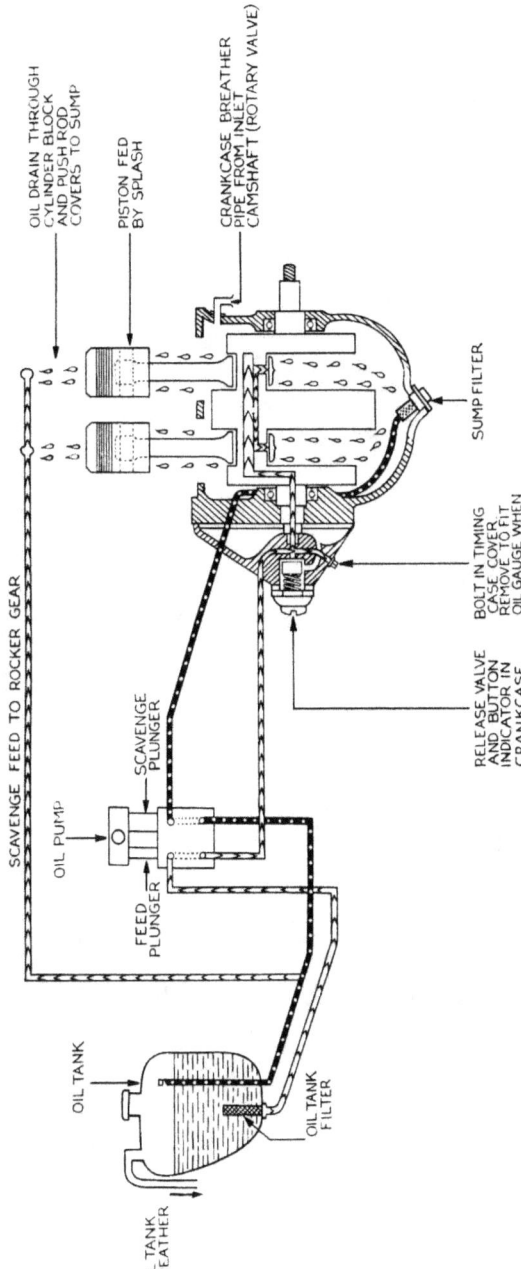

Fig. 12. Diagram of lubrication system (1963–69 650 c.c. unit-construction models 6T, TR6, TR6S/S and T120)

The system on 1956–62 500 and 650c.c. models 5T, 6T, TR5, TR6, T100, T110 and T120 without unit-construction is similar to the above except for some variations in tank filter and sump filter design. All 1966–69 models have rear chain lubrication as indicated in Fig. 13

(From Triumph Workshop Manual)

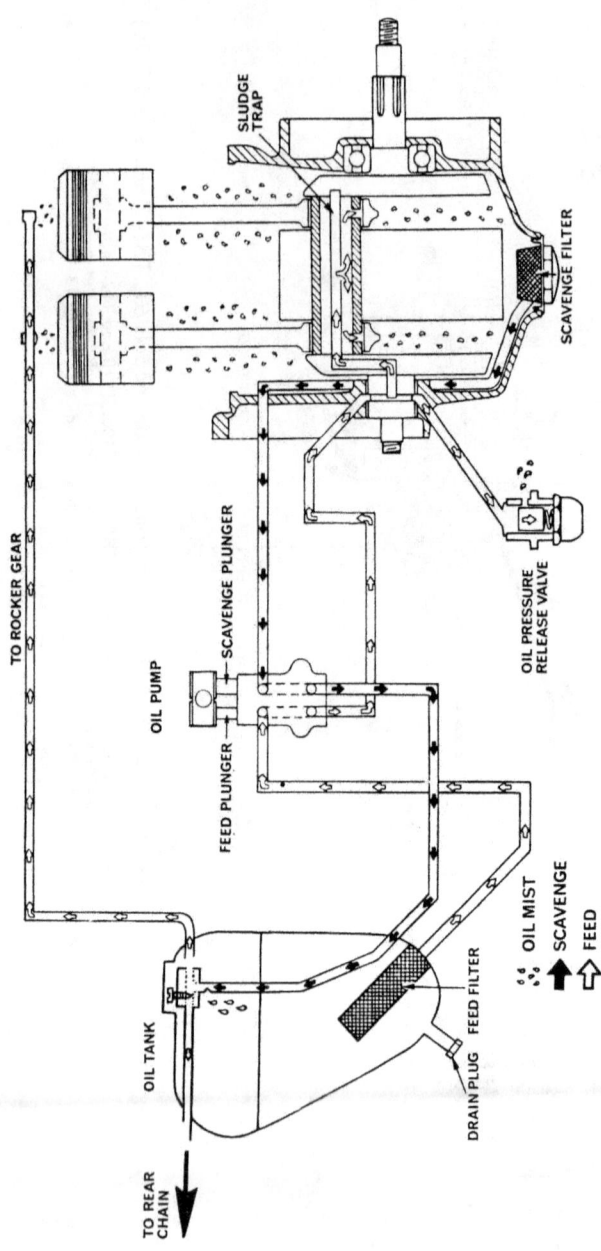

Fig. 13. Diagram of lubrication system (1961–69 350 and 500 c.c. unit-construction models 3TA, 5TA, T90, T100A and T100S/S)

On all 1956–65 350 and 500 c.c. models prior to engine No. H 40528 the oil-pressure release valve incorporates an indicator button as shown in Fig. 14 and an oil supply to the rear chain from the oil return pipe is not provided as shown above. See also caption to Fig. 56

(*From Triumph Workshop Manual*)

valve cap (4). As the engine r.p.m. approach 2,000 (equivalent to about 30 m.p.h. in top gear) the button should just commence to protrude thereby indicating that the oil pressure between the oil pump and the crankshaft is normal. Above 2,000 engine r.p.m. the button should remain *fully* protruded, indicating that excessive oil pressure is being effectively released.

On all 350 and 500 c.c. engines from engine No. H 40528 the oil-pressure release valve, as may be seen in Fig. 15, has no indicator shaft and button. In this case to check the oil circulation, remove the oil tank filler cap and observe whether, with the engine running, an intermittent stream of oil flows from the end of the oil-return pipe. Small bubbles should cover the surface of the oil inside the tank. Where no indicator shaft and button are provided, make a habit of checking the oil circulation in this manner before starting out on every long run. Note that for some minutes after starting up the engine it is quite usual for an excessive amount of oil to flow from the return pipe. The flow should then be normal.

If an Oil Pressure Gauge is Fitted. With the engine cold the gauge should read about 80 lb. per sq. in., and with the engine hot about 30 lb. per sq. in. On 1969 models a red warning light in the headlamp top-face shows when pressure falls to about 7 lb. per sq. in.

Change Engine Oil and Clean Tank Filter Every 1,500 Miles. This should also be done while running-in a new or rebored engine after covering the first 250, 500 and 1,000 miles. When the engine is hot most of the foreign matter is in suspension and it is therefore always advisable to drain the oil tank, clean its filter and replenish with fresh engine oil *after* a run.

On Triumph Twins fitted with rear enclosure panels it is necessary, except on certain models, to remove the off-side panel in order to drain the oil tank and remove the filter for cleaning. Panel removal is simple, but on most 650 c.c. unit-construction models its removal necessitates unscrewing two domed nuts, a plain nut below the rear of the petrol tank, and two front panel junction screws.

To drain the oil tank, remove its filler cap, place a drip-tray beneath the oil tank, remove the drain plug from the bottom of the tank, and allow the warm oil to drain off for about ten minutes. Some models have no separate drain plug fitted as shown in Fig. 13 and in this case it is necessary to unscrew the union nut and disconnect the oil feed pipe (the bottom one) from the oil tank. This must, of course, be done in order to remove the gauze filter shown in Figs. 12 and 13. Afterwards unscrew the large hexagonal nut to which the filter is attached, withdraw the unit, and then thoroughly clean it in paraffin (kerosene).

Before changing the engine oil it is advisable to flush out the tank with a proprietary flushing oil (obtainable from most garages and accessory firms). If this is not available, use paraffin as an alternative, being careful to remove all trace of it afterwards. If the oil tank is found to be very dirty, disconnect the oil-return pipe as well as the delivery pipe, remove the oil tank from the motor-cycle, and clean it very thoroughly.

When replacing the gauze filter see that the fibre washer above the hexagonal nut is in good condition and when re-connecting the oil feed-pipe union nut avoid excessive tightening. Replace the separate drain plug (where fitted), replenish the oil tank with about 5 pints of suitable engine oil (*see* page 26) to within $1\frac{1}{2}$ in. of the filler cap. When you have re-started the engine check that oil circulation is satisfactory (*see* page 26) and that no oil leakage occurs.

Drain Sump and Clean its Filter When Changing Engine Oil. On all engines a gauze filter, combined or integral with the sump drain plate or plug, is located at the base of the crankcase and it should be removed and cleaned thoroughly in paraffin (kerosene) during each oil change when the engine is hot. Allow all oil to drain from the engine sump for about ten minutes.

On earlier engines (mostly not of the unit-construction type) the gauze filter and its cover plate can be removed from the sump by unscrewing the four plate-securing nuts. When withdrawing the unit be careful not to damage the filter gauze.

On most later engines (including nearly all those of unit-construction type) the hexagon-headed sump drain-plug housing the gauze filter is located near the crankcase bottom mounting lug and can be readily removed with the appropriate spanner.

Whatever type of sump filter unit is provided, when replacing it see that its joint washer is sound and that the unit is firmly secured to the crank-case. Where the filter unit includes a plate, tighten its securing nuts firmly and evenly in a diagonal order.

Maintenance of Oil-pressure Release Valve. Two types of valve (*see* Figs. 14 and 15) are fitted and both are similar except that one has no indicator shaft and button for visual checking of the oil pressure and circulation. Both types are thoroughly reliable and require no mainten-ance other than occasional cleaning. When changing the engine oil, or perhaps at somewhat less frequent intervals, it is desirable to remove and strip down the release-valve unit, clean all of its components thoroughly in paraffin (kerosene), inspect them for wear, and then reassemble and replace the unit.

After cleaning the various components check that the piston (*9*) slides freely in the valve body (*11*). Also see that the cone-shaped filter on the end of the valve body is not damaged or obstructed and that the piston is not scored. Appreciable scoring affects oil pressure. In no circumstances tamper with the release-valve spring or springs. Their poundage is set to give the correct oil pressure. If spring renewal becomes necessary, use only genuine Triumph spares.

TRIUMPH LUBRICATION   31

To Dismantle and Assemble Oil-pressure Release Valve (Fig. 14). To remove the complete unit from the crankcase, remove the hexagonal nut adjacent to the crankcase surface, and withdraw the unit. To dismantle the unit unscrew the valve cap (*4*) from the valve body (*11*), holding the

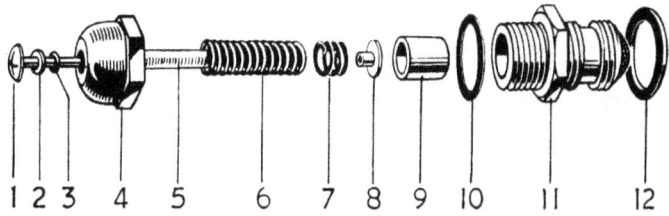

Fig. 14. Exploded view of oil-pressure release valve provided with indicator shaft and button

Fitted to all 650 c.c. and all earlier 350 and 500 c.c. engines (see page 27)

(*From Triumph Workshop Manual*)

Key to Figs. 14, 15

1. Button of indicator shaft
2. Retaining cup for 3
3. Rubber oil seal
4. Valve cap
5. Rubber sleeve
6. Main spring
7. Auxiliary spring
8. Brass indicator-shaft nut
9. Piston
10. Fibre washer for 4
11. Valve body
12. Fibre washer for 11

latter with a spanner, and remove the piston (*9*). Then remove the brass indicator-shaft nut (*8*) and withdraw the main spring (*6*), the auxiliary spring (*7*), the rubber sleeve (*5*) and the indicator shaft and button (*1*).

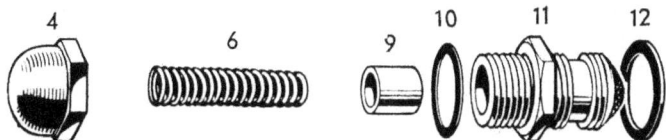

Fig. 15. Exploded view of oil-pressure release valve not provided with indicator shaft and button

Fitted to all later 350 and 500 c.c. engines (see page 28)

(*From Triumph Workshop Manual*)

Lever out the retaining cup (*2*) from the valve cap (*4*) and remove the rubber oil seal (*3*).

To assemble the oil-pressure release valve unit, first press the rubber oil seal (*3*) and retaining cup (*2*) into the valve cap (*4*). Next slide the rubber sleeve (*5*) over the indicator shaft (*1*) and press the sleeve over the stub on the inside of the valve cap. Then position the indicator shaft (*1*) correctly and replace the main spring (*6*) and the auxiliary spring (*7*). Afterwards screw home the brass indicator-shaft nut (*8*). Finally offer up the piston (*9*) into the valve body (*11*), renew the fibre washer (*10*) and screw the valve cap on to the valve body. Tighten the cap firmly but, when doing this, do not hold the valve body in a vice as this can cause distortion and serious damage. When screwing the oil-pressure release valve unit home into the crankcase, fit a new fibre joint washer between the crankcase and the valve body, and tighten the unit securing nut very firmly.

To Dismantle and Assemble Oil-pressure Release Valve (Fig. 15). The dismantling and assembling procedure for an oil-pressure release valve unit not provided with a button indicator is the same as that just described for a unit with a button indicator except for reference to six components not fitted, i.e. those numbered 1-3, 5, 7, 8 in Fig. 14.

The Triumph Oil Pump. The double-plunger-type pump (*see* Fig. 11) located inside the timing cover has its drive-block slider driven by an eccentric peg on the nut fitted to the end of the inlet camshaft. It rarely requires any maintenance.

The drive-block slider is made of aluminium and is the only part likely to wear even after a big mileage. When appreciable wear does eventually occur on its bore and in the plunger cross-head, renew the slider. The oil pump body and the scavenge and feed plungers are always immersed in engine oil when the engine is running and wear of these components is therefore extremely slow.

Should the two non-return valve balls fail to seat properly in the ball-valve seatings, the oil pump will cease to circulate the oil satisfactorily. To remedy this trouble, remove the oil pump as described below. Then remove both body plugs and withdraw the ball-valve springs and the pump-valve balls. Wash all parts thoroughly in paraffin (kerosene) to remove foreign matter, and when replacing the balls on their seatings give them a sharp tap.

Removing and Replacing Oil Pump. After removing the timing cover from the engine, remove the two conical nuts securing the oil pump unit and withdraw it from its mounting studs. Prime the oil pump before replacing it, and fit a new pump gasket. When fitting and tightening the two conical nuts securing the oil pump unit, make sure that the cones of the nuts and washers fit properly into the countersunk holes of the oil pump body. Also when replacing the timing cover, see that the joint faces are quite clean before applying some jointing compound.

Oil Pipes (Tank to Engine). Care must be exercised when replacing the rubber connexions of any oil pipes so that any inside chafing is prevented. If chafing occurs, it is possible that a small piece of rubber may enter the oil system and this, on reaching the oil pump, would cause lack of pressure to the crankshaft. Any foreign matter in the scavenge pipe-line above the pump is returned to the oil tank (the rocker oil feed may be blocked in exceptional cases) and is prevented from entering the oil system by the tank filter.

Valve Rockers, Rocker Spindles and Push-rods. The oil feed to the rocker spindles is supplied by the scavenge side of the main oil-supply. The only thing which can cause a lack of oil to the rockers is a stoppage in the oil pipe-line. This can be rectified by removing the pipe and checking by forcing air through it. To check the oil supply at the spindles, run the engine until it is warm so that the oil temperature is increased and then slacken off the two acorn nuts, which secure the oil pipe banjos to the rocker spindles, when a regular drip of oil should continue. If the motor-cycle has been "laid-up" for some time, it is advantageous to flood the rocker mechanism. Start the engine, remove the oil tank filler cap, and then place a finger over the scavenge outlet pipe so that the oil is forced through the rocker spindles, rockers and to the push-rods.

Dynamo and Magneto Lubrication. For lighting and ignition a Lucas dynamo and an independent Lucas magneto are provided on earlier Triumph Twins not fitted with a Lucas a.c./d.c. lighting-ignition system and their lubrication is dealt with on page 44.

Lubrication of Contact-breaker (Coil Ignition Models). For instructions on lubricating the contact-breaker, combined with the distributor unit at the rear of the engine or located separately on the off-side of the engine, *see* pages 50–53 and 55 or 126 respectively.

MOTOR-CYCLE LUBRICATION

Topping-up the Gearbox. On pre-unit-construction Triumphs it is advisable to top-up the gearbox as required to the correct level about every 1,000 miles. To do this, remove the filler plug and the level plug shown in Fig. 16 and, after placing a drip-tray beneath the gearbox, pour in suitable oil (*see* later paragraph) until it begins to trickle from the orifice for the level plug. In no circumstances lubricate any Triumph gearbox with a heavy viscous oil or grease. When dripping of oil ceases, replace the level plug and its washer, followed by the filler plug. Be sure to tighten the level plug securely.

On 350 and 500 c.c. unit-construction models also top-up the gearbox as required to the correct level about every 1,000 miles; in the case of 650 c.c. unit-construction models topping-up about every 3,000 miles is recommended. On *all* unit-construction Triumph models the oil-level plug is screwed into the drain plug (which has a level tube) as illustrated in Fig. 17. To top-up the gearbox correctly, remove the oil-filler plug from the top of the gearbox, adjacent to the clutch-cable abutment, and also remove the level plug (the smaller of the two). Then pour in suitable oil (page 35) until it begins to drip from the hole in the drain plug. The

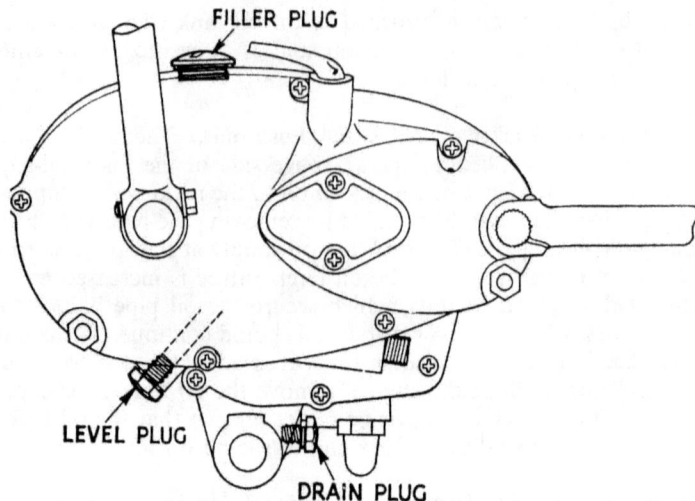

Fig. 16. Showing location of gearbox plugs on all pre-unit-construction Triumphs

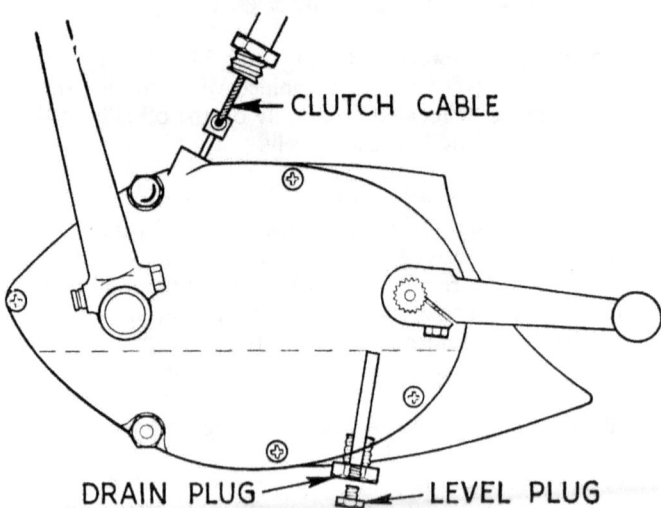

Fig. 17. The correct gearbox oil level and the level tube, level plug and drain plug assembly on unit-construction Triumphs

On 350 and 500 c.c. models the oil level and drain plug assembly is positioned vertically, and the clutch-cable abutment on top of the gearbox is towards the front and not the rear

gearbox oil level will then be correct as indicated by the dotted line shown in Fig. 17. When oil dripping ceases, replace the level plug and tighten it firmly.

TRIUMPH LUBRICATION

Suitable Oils for Gearbox Lubrication. Those recommended for summer and winter use when riding in the U.K. or Overseas are—
1 Castrol Grand Prix.
2 Mobiloil D.
3 B.P. Energol SAE.50.
4 Shell X-100 50.
5 Esso Extra Motor Oil 50.
6 Regent Havoline SAE.50.

Changing the Gearbox Oil. In the case of a new or reconditioned gearbox you are advised to do this after the first 500 miles, and subsequently about every 6,000 miles. On unit-construction models it is a good plan to do this after a run when the oil is warm. Quick and thorough draining is thereby made easier.

On pre-unit construction models, referring to Fig. 16, remove the filler plug, the level plug, and the drain plug and allow all oil to drain into a suitable receptacle. Then flush out the gearbox, replace the drain plug, and replenish with suitable oil to the correct level as previously described for topping-up the gearbox.

On all unit-construction models, referring to Fig. 17, remove the filler plug on top of the gearbox and also the complete assembly comprising the drain plug, the level tube and the level plug. Drain the gearbox completely, flush it out, replace the drain plug with the level plug removed, and then replenish the gearbox as previously described for topping-up. Finally replace the level plug.

Lubrication of Clutch, etc. The Triumph clutch is a multi-plate design with synthetic friction inserts in its driven plates and a transmission shock absorber included. It is designed to function *in oil* and to ensure smooth and easy operation, and to prevent the friction inserts becoming burnt or damaged when the clutch is under heavy load, it is absolutely essential to drain and replenish the oil-bath chain case with suitable oil to the correct level at regular intervals. On all later unit-construction models frequent topping-up is also recommended. The maintenance of sufficient lubricant in the oil-bath chain case besides being vital for clutch operation, is also necessary to prevent excessive noise, wear of the primary chain and, in the case of all coil-ignition models, possible damage to the alternator unit.

Suitable Oils for Oil-bath Chain Case (All Models). The Triumph Engineering Co. Ltd. recommend for summer and winter use in the U.K. one of the following lubricants—
1 Castrol Castrolite.
2 Shell X-100 20W.
3 B.P. Energol SAE.20.
4 Mobiloil Arctic.
5 Esso Extra Motor Oil 20W/30.
6 Regent Havoline SAE.20W.

Replenishing Oil-bath Chain Case (Pre-unit-construction Models). On the 1956–62 "B" range of 500 and 650 c.c. Triumph Twins, drain and refill the oil-bath chain case every 1,000 miles, preferably *after* a run when the oil is fairly warm. Place a drip-tray below the oil drain plug (located below the middle of the chain-case cover), remove the filler plug and the drain plug, and allow all oil to drain off. Replace and firmly tighten the drain plug and then replenish the oil-bath chain case with ¼ pint (150 c.c.)

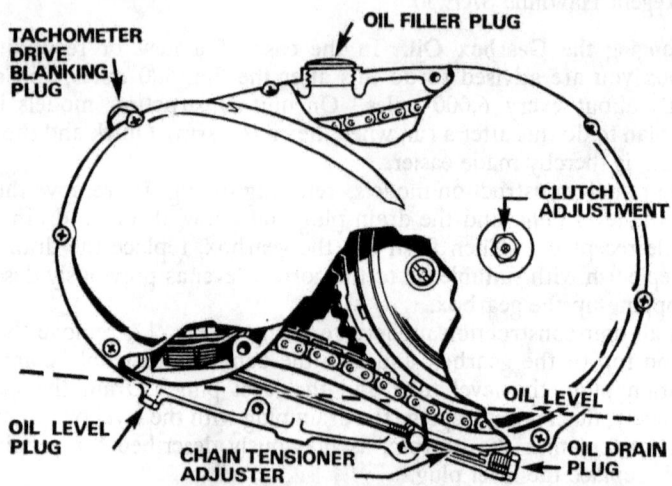

Fig. 18. Details of oil-bath chain case fitted to most 350 and 500 c.c. unit-construction Triumph Twins

The design illustrated applies to all 1965–69 350, 500 c.c. models from engine No. H 40528
(*From Triumph Workshop Manual*)

of one of the oils previously recommended. If any oil leakage occurs, check that the drain plug washer has been replaced and that the screws which secure the chain-case cover are tight.

Topping-up and Replenishing Oil-bath Chain Case (All Unit-construction Models). On many earlier 350 and 500 c.c. models an oil level plug is not provided as on later models (*see* Fig. 18). In this case drain and replenish the oil-bath chain case every 1,000 miles as previously described for pre-unit construction models, but replenish with ½ pint (300 c.c.) of recommended oil instead of with ¼ pint (150 c.c.). This will ensure the oil level being correct.

On all later 350, 500 and 650 c.c. models having an oil-bath chain case provided with an oil level plug as shown in Figs. 18 or 19, top-up the oil-bath chain case, if necessary, every 250 miles and drain and replenish it every 1,000 miles.

To top-up the chain case remove the oil-level plug located at the front or rear (*see* Figs. 18 or 19) and then pour in oil through the oil filler-plug orifice until it begins to trickle from the hole for the oil-level plug. When oil ceases to emerge, replace and firmly tighten the oil-level plug.

To drain and replenish the oil-bath chain case on 350, 500 and 650 c.c. models with the type of case shown in Figs. 18 or 19, first remove the oil-drain plug (which also gives access to the chain tensioner) from the base of the chain case close to the near-side footrest. On some of the earlier

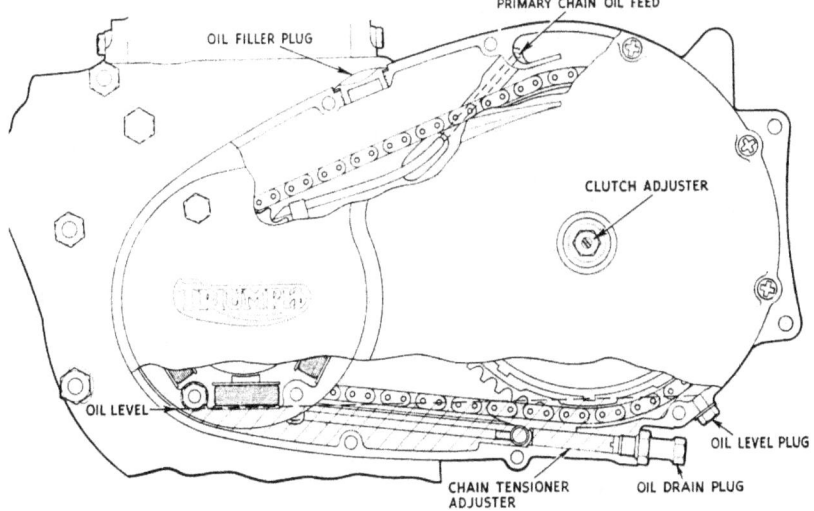

Fig. 19. Details of oil-bath chain case fitted to 650 c.c. unit-construction models

This arrangement applies to all 1963-69 650 c.c. models from engine No. DU 101 onwards
(From Triumph Workshop Manual)

350 and 500 c.c. models it may be necessary first to slacken the near-side footrest by loosening its mounting bolt and tapping the footrest sharply downwards to free it from its locking taper. Having removed the drain plug, allow the oil (preferably warm after a run) to drain away for about 10 minutes. Then replace the drain plug and its fibre washer, firmly tighten the plug, remove the oil-level plug, and then pour in recommended oil (*see* page 35) through the oil filler-plug orifice (adjacent to the cylinder block base) or through the clutch adjustment-nut aperture (in the centre of the chain-case outer cover) until oil commences to trickle from the hole for the oil-level plug. The oil level is then correct, and the plug can be replaced and firmly tightened. Do not forget to replace its washer.

When topping-up or replenishing the oil-bath chain case it is, of course, necessary when making use of the oil-level plug to determine the correct oil level, to keep the motor-cycle *level* and not tilted. If draining and replenishment are effected without removing the oil-level plug, to obtain the correct oil level pour in ½ pint (300 c.c.) of oil for a 350 or 500 c.c. model, or ⅝ pint (350 c.c.) in the case of a 650 c.c. Triumph model.

The Secondary Chain. On all 1956 and later Triumph Twins some automatic lubrication of this is provided. On most models it takes the form of oil splash from the oil-bath chain case, and on some models an adjustable needle-valve is provided on its outer cover. Where such is fitted, screw the valve out or in to increase or decrease the oil supply respectively.

On 1966 and later 350 and 500 c.c. unit-construction models a positive oil feed is taken from the oil-return pipe inside the oil tank as shown in Fig. 13. To adjust the oil supply for the secondary chain, remove the oil-tank filler-cap and turn the adjuster screw in the neck of the tank clockwise or anti-clockwise as required to reduce or increase the rate of oil flow respectively.

However, irrespective of the design of automatic lubrication provided for the secondary chain, especially where the latter is not fully enclosed, some regular manual lubrication of the chain is essential to maintain it and the sprocket teeth in good condition.

About every 250 miles, or whenever the chain appears to be in a dry state, apply some engine oil (*see* page 26) or graphite grease with an oil-can or stiff brush to the lower chain run while slowly turning the rear wheel over by hand. If you use an oil-can, see that the oil falls upon the bearing surfaces and not only on the rollers. Where the secondary chain is protected only by a chain guard, it is preferable always to apply graphite grease. In addition to giving your chain the above treatment, you are strongly advised about every 1,000 miles in wet weather, and about every 1,500 miles in dry weather, to clean and lubricate it in the following manner—

1 Disconnect the connecting link and withdraw the chain from the gearbox and rear-wheel sprockets.
2 With a suitable wire brush remove all grit, road dust, etc., from the chain and clean it by immersion in a paraffin or kerosene bath.
3 Hang up the chain on a nail and allow all paraffin or kerosene to drain off.
4 Immerse the chain for about 15 minutes in a suitable receptacle containing Castrolease Graphited, Mobilgrease No. 2, B.P. Energrease A.O., or Esso Fluid Grease, melted over a low flame, or to be on the safe side, over a pan of boiling water. Move the chain about occasionally to facilitate penetration of the grease into its roller bearings.
5 Allow the grease to cool, remove the chain from its grease receptacle, and wipe off all surplus grease.
6 Replace the secondary chain on the gearbox and rear wheel sprockets and connect its ends. When doing this, make quite sure that the open

TRIUMPH LUBRICATION

end of the spring link faces *away from* the direction of chain movement. This is most important.

Use of Grease-gun. The standard Triumph tool-kit does not include a grease-gun and it is advisable to use a good proprietary high-pressure type such as the Tecalemit for greasing those items provided with grease nipples. These items include the front- and rear-brake camshafts and the swinging-arm fork for the rear suspension, but not the wheel bearings and steering head.

For charging a grease-gun quickly it is best to use the modern type grease canister having a loose collar provided with a hole. To charge a grease-gun with this type of canister, remove the screwed nozzle-cap from the gun, place the barrel of the gun over the hole in the central floating plate of the canister, and press down firmly. Turn the grease-gun and simultaneously remove it from the floating plate. The grease-gun should then be fully charged, i.e. with the grease flush with the top of the barrel. Before using the gun, see that its nozzle cap is firmly screwed down.

The main advantage of using a modern type canister is, of course, that it eliminates the rather messy job of filling the grease-gun by hand, using a lath or similar implement.

Greases Recommended for Use. Six greases recommended by the Triumph Engineering Co. Ltd. for application with the grease-gun to nipples provided for lubricating the rear-brake pedal spindle, and for repacking the bearings of the wheel bearings and steering head are as follows—
1 Castrolease LM;
2 Shell Retinax A;
3 B.P. Energrease L2;
4 Mobilgrease MP;
5 Esso Multipurpose Grease H;
6 Regent Marfak Multipurpose 2.

The All-important Brakes. Every 1,000 miles apply with an oil-can a few drops of oil to the yoke-end pins at the front and rear ends of the rear-brake rod. Do not overlook the threaded portion of this rod to which the hand adjuster is fitted. Also do not disregard the exposed ends of the front-brake cable.

Every 1,000 miles grease the front and rear brake-camshafts. A grease nipple is provided at the end of each camshaft and is integral with it. To prevent grease getting on the brake-shoe linings, apply the grease sparingly; one stroke should normally be sufficient. Should grease fail to penetrate when greasing a camshaft, remove the latter and clean it thoroughly in paraffin. During reassembly grease the cam bearing surfaces.

Every 3,000 miles grease the rear-brake pedal spindle. No grease nipple is provided and it is necessary to remove the brake pedal and then grease its spindle.

Slacken the hand adjuster-nut on the rear-brake rod, unscrew the pedal retaining nut, and then remove the pedal from the spindle. With some fine emery cloth remove any rust from the latter, clean the spindle and the pedal bore and after smearing some grease on the spindle, replace the pedal, the spring and plain washers, and the pedal retaining nut. Firmly tighten this nut.

Grease Hub Bearings Every 12,000 Miles. Journal ball bearings are fitted to the hubs of both wheels and on all new machines are packed with grease. Every 12,000 miles remove both wheels, dismantle their hubs and repack the bearings with a recommended type grease (*see* page 39). For detailed instructions on dismantling the hubs, greasing the bearings and correct reassembly procedure, you are advised to refer to the appropriate *Triumph Workshop Manual*.

The Triumph Rear Suspension. The Girling hydraulic-type rear suspension units are sealed by their makers and require no topping-up with hydraulic fluid by the motor-cyclist. The swinging fork (often called the "swinging arm"), however, does need some lubrication.

Fig. 20. Showing (arrowed) the location of the grease nipple on the swinging fork

The nipple is similarly positioned on all 1956 and later Triumph Twins, but on 650 c.c. unit-construction models it is below the off-side swinging-fork lug
(*From Triumph Workshop Manual*)

The grease nipple for the swinging fork is provided underneath the latter in a fairly central position as indicated in Fig. 20. Every 1,000 miles (every 1,500 miles on unit-construction models) apply the grease-gun to the nipple until grease is forced through each end of the pivot bearings.

TRIUMPH LUBRICATION   41

If grease fails to penetrate, you must remove the swinging-fork pivot to ensure adequate lubrication.

The Telescopic Front Forks. Every 6,000 miles drain and replenish the fork legs as described on page 69. Engine oil (*see* page 26) should be used for replenishment, and be sure to replenish with the correct grade during the winter. *See* also page 130 for 1968–9 fork details.

Steering Head. This has no grease nipples provided. On a new Triumph Twin the races of the ball bearings are packed with grease. Every 12,000 miles it is advisable to remove and partially dismantle the telescopic front-fork unit, and then repack the steering head bearings with the recommended type grease (*see* page 39). This should be done after cleaning the cups and cones thoroughly with paraffin. For correct dismantling, greasing and assembly procedure, see the appropriate *Triumph Workshop Manual*.

Control Levers, Joints and Exposed Cables. To prevent corrosion, and to ensure smooth action, every 1,000 miles apply a few drops of engine oil (*see* page 26) with an oil-can to all these items. A more thorough and long-term method of oiling a control cable connected to a handlebar lever is as follows.

Disconnect the Bowden cable connexion from the handlebar control, and with some brown paper make a suitable funnel; attach this to the cable casing, using a rubber band to secure it. Then pour some engine oil into the funnel and allow this to trickle overnight down between the casing and cable. Keep all control cables well clear of the upper part of the power unit, otherwise the oil in the cables casings will gradually dry up. The throttle twist-grip, by the way, normally requires no lubrication.

The Dipper Switch. Every 5,000 miles lubricate the moving parts of the dipper switch with a little *thin* oil. Do not apply more than a few drops, otherwise a short-circuit may occur.

Speedometer Cable. It is advisable about every 12,000 miles to grease the speedometer-drive cable. Disconnect it from the speedometer unit and withdraw the inner cable. On nacelle models it is first necessary to remove the Lucas headlamp unit by loosening the securing screw located close to the speedometer on the nacelle. Now unscrew the union nut at the speedometer base, withdraw the inner cable, and then clean it thoroughly with paraffin. Smear the cable (except for the last 6 in. at the speedometer end) sparingly with suitable grease (*see* page 39) and insert the cable into its casing. Wipe off all surplus grease and make sure that both "squared" ends of the inner cable are located in their "square" drive-housings before tightening the union nut.

Where a Sidecar is Attached. Do not forget to grease the hub bearings of the sidecar wheel, and attend to any other lubrication points in accordance with the instructions issued by the makers of the sidecar fitted.

Easing Rusted Parts. Rusted items, such as bolts or nuts, on the engine or on the motor-cycle itself can usually be eased by the application of one of the following six oils: Shell Donax P; Mobil Spring Oil; B.P. Energol; Castrol; Esso or Regent Graphited, "Penetrating Oil."

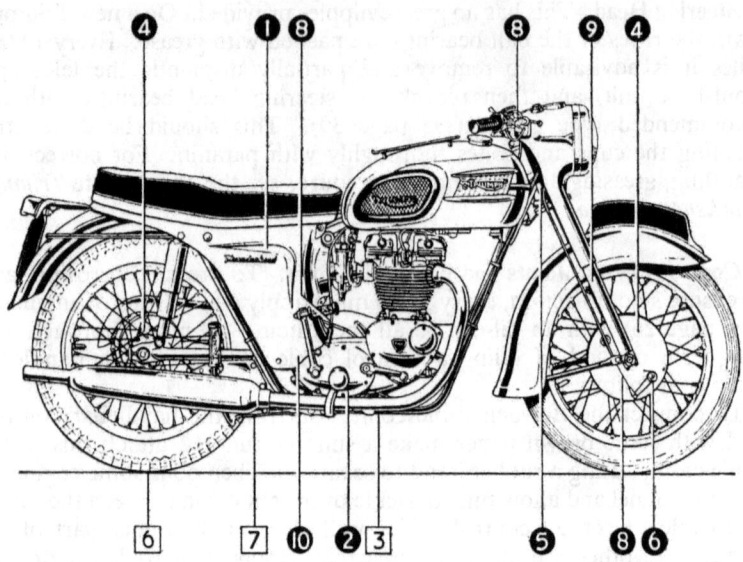

Fig. 21. Lubrication chart showing items requiring regular attention

This chart (illustrating a 650 c.c. unit-construction model) and the more detailed key below apply to all 1956 and later 350, 500 and 650 c.c. Triumph Twins, although the design of some items illustrated varies, of course, to some extent on different models. Note that the numbered items with a black background have lubrication points near or on the off-side of the motor-cycle, the remainder being on the near-side.

Item No.	Description of Item	Page Ref.	Item No.	Description of Item	Page Ref.
1.	Oil tank	26	5.	Steering head	41
—	Filters	29, 30	6.	Brake camshaft	39
—	Oil-pressure release valve	30–32	7.	Brake pedal spindle	39
—	Contact-breaker	50, 55	8.	Controls and cables	41
2.	Gearbox	33	—	Dipper switch	41
3.	Oil-bath chain case	36	9.	Telescopic forks	69
—	Secondary chain	38	10.	Rear suspension	40
4.	Wheel hubs	40	—	Speedometer cable	41

4 Lighting and Ignition Systems

Automatic Voltage Control. Where automatic voltage control is provided (1956 to 1959), the cut-out and regulator are combined as a unit separate from the dynamo. The regulator which is connected across the dynamo brushes dispenses with the "third brush" and operates on the "trembler" principle, automatically varying the output of the dynamo according to the state of charge of the battery and the load. Thus, charging is purely automatic and not under the control of the rider.

Where automatic voltage control is provided (magneto models) there are only three switch positions, namely, "OFF," "L," and "H." In all three positions the dynamo gives a controlled output as already explained. During daylight running with the battery well charged the dynamo gives only a trickle charge and the ammeter may show only 1 or 2 amperes.

The Headlamp. The headlamp is fitted with a double-filament bulb; one filament is arranged to be approximately at the focus of the reflector and gives the normal driving light, while the second one, mounted slightly above the other, gives a dipped, anti-dazzling beam for use when meeting traffic or driving in mist or fog, this device being controlled by a switch mounted on the handlebars. A small pilot bulb is also provided for use when the machine is stationary, and for town riding.

The Ammeter. This instrument shows the amount of current flowing into or from the battery; it gives an indication that the equipment is working in a satisfactory manner.

THE LUCAS DYNAMO (1956–59)

On models with Lucas dynamo lighting the equipment comprises the following.

Dynamo Output Control. The dynamo works in conjunction with a regulator unit to give compensated voltage control, but the regulator and cut-out are electrically separate, although combined structurally. Neither should be tampered with as they are both properly adjusted during manufacture.

The regulator provides a completely automatic control. The dynamo output varies according to the load on the battery and its state of charge—the dynamo gives a high output when the battery is discharged, and a trickle-charge only when the battery is fully charged so as to keep the battery in good condition. The regulator also provides increased output when current is taken by the lamps.

The cut-out is an automatic switch. It connects the dynamo to the battery only when the dynamo voltage is higher than the battery voltage, and disconnects to prevent the battery discharging through the dynamo windings.

The dynamo output is correctly set to suit the requirements of the motor-cycle and under normal conditions the battery will be kept in good order.

Ammeter Readings. During daytime running, when the battery is in good condition, the dynamo gives only a trickle charge and the ammeter needle shows only a small deflection to the "+" side of the scale.

When the headlamp is switched on, a discharge reading is shown when the battery voltage is high; after a short time the battery voltage drops and the regulator responds so that the dynamo output balances the lamp load.

Lubrication. As grease-packed ball bearings are fitted at both ends, no lubrication is required until the machine is taken down for a general overhaul.

Inspection of Brushgear and Commutator. At six-monthly intervals remove the commutator cover and examine the brushgear and commutator. The brushes—held in boxes by means of springs—must make firm contact with the commutator; see that each brush is free to slide in its holder. If it is sticking, remove and clean with a petrol-moistened cloth. When replacing the brushes each one must be returned to its original position so that it "beds" properly on the commutator. Replace brushes if they are badly worn, but fitting by a Service Agent is desirable to ensure that they "bed" properly on the commutator (*see* Fig. 22).

To function efficiently the commutator should be free from any trace of oil or dirt and should appear highly polished. If dirty or blackened, clean it by pressing a clean, dry cloth against it while the engine is slowly turned over by means of the kickstarter; if very dirty, use a petrol-moistened cloth.

THE LUCAS MAGNETO (1956–59)

Where a Triumph is equipped with magneto ignition a rotating-armature pattern magneto is employed. This has the magnet cast into the body; this eliminates joints and improves the weatherproof properties of the magneto. The ignition timing is dealt with on page 96.

Lubrication. Lubrication is advised about every 3,000 miles. The cam is

LIGHTING AND IGNITION SYSTEMS

supplied with lubricant from a felt pad in a pocket in the contact-breaker housing. A wick in a small hole in the cam allows the oil to find its way to the surface of the cam. To lubricate, remove the contact-breaker cover, turn the engine over until the hole in the cam is seen, then carefully add a few drops of thin machine oil. No oil must be allowed to get on or near the contacts (*see* Fig. 23) of a Lucas K2F or K2FC magneto.

The contact-breaker rocker-arm pivot should also be lubricated. The complete contact-breaker must be removed for this purpose. To do this, take out the hexagon-headed screw from the centre of the contact-breaker

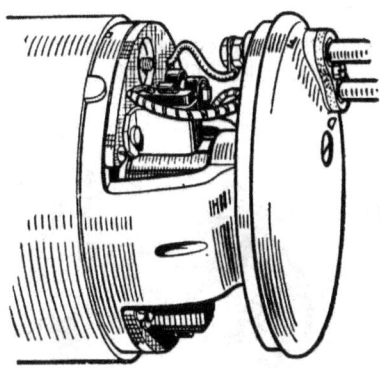

Fig. 22. Commutator end of Lucas dynamo with cover band removed (1956–59 models)

and lever the contact-breaker carefully off the tapered shaft on which it fits, push aside the rocker-arm retaining spring, lift off the rocker arm and smear the pivot with a little Mobilgrease No. 2 or similar grease.

The cam ring which is a sliding fit in its housing should be removed and the inside and outside surfaces lightly smeared with Mobilgrease No. 2. If the handlebar ignition lever is half retarded, removal and re-fitting the cam is rendered more easy. Apply one or two drops of thin machine-oil to the felt cam-lubricator in the housing. Then re-fit the cam, taking care that the stop peg in the housing and the timing-control plunger engage with their respective slots.

In some cases an earthing brush is fitted at the back of the contact-breaker base; see that it is clean and has free movement in its holder before re-fitting. When replacing the contact-breaker, be careful to see that the projecting key on the tapered portion of the contact-breaker case engages with the keyway cut in the magneto spindle. Replace the contact-breaker securing screw and tighten with care, otherwise ignition timing will be affected.

The bearings of the armature are packed with grease by the makers. When the machine is dismantled for general overhaul it is advisable to have the magneto inspected by a Lucas Service Depot or Agent.

Adjustment of Contact-breaker Gap. Check the setting of the contact-breaker every 3,000 miles. To check, remove the contact-breaker cover and turn the engine until the contacts are fully open. A feeler gauge should be used for checking the gap—the gauge should have a thickness of 0·012 in.–0·015 in. (0·30–0·40 mm). A suitable gauge is provided on the magneto spanner. It should be a sliding fit if the gap is correct; adjust the setting if the gap varies appreciably from that recommended. To do this, with the engine in the position which gives maximum separation, slacken the lock-nut and turn the contact screw by its hexagon head until the gap is properly adjusted. Tighten the lock-nut and re-check the gap.

Cleaning Contacts. Take off the contact-breaker cover and examine the contact-breaker every 6,000 miles. Clean dirty or pitted contacts with a

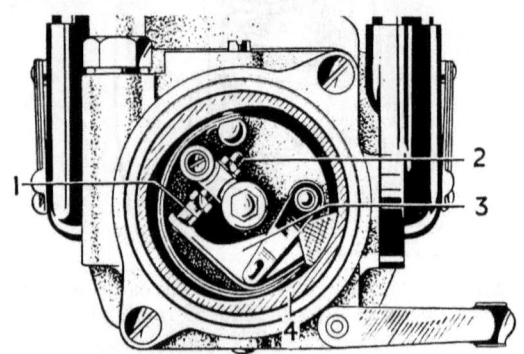

Fig. 23. Showing contact-breaker of Lucas magneto fitted to 1956–59 pre-unit-construction models

Applicable to Models TR5, TR6, T100, T110 and T120

1. Contacts (closed)
2. Fixed-contact screw and lock-nut
3. Rocker arm and integral moving-contact
4. Cam ring (with manual control)

fine carborundum stone or, if not available, with very fine emery cloth. Wipe away any dirt or metal dust with a petrol-moistened cloth. Remove any rust from the contact-breaker springs. When cleaned, check the contact-breaker gap (*see* Fig. 23).

To remove the contacts for cleaning, unscrew the contact-breaker securing screw. Lever the contact-breaker off its tapered shaft, push the locating spring to the side and lift the rocker arm off its pivot; it is then possible to get at the contacts to clean them. Check the projecting key on the tapered portion of the contact-breaker base, when replacing the contact-breaker, and see that it engages with the keyway cut in the armature spindle. Replace the contact-breaker securing screw and tighten carefully.

High-tension Pick-up. Remove this after approximately every 6,000

LIGHTING AND IGNITION SYSTEMS 47

miles running. Wipe the moulding with a clean, dry cloth, then check that the carbon brush has free movement in its holder, but be careful not to over-stretch the brush spring. Clean the brush if dirty, using a petrol-moistened cloth. A brush worn, say, to within $\frac{1}{8}$ in. (3·0 mm) of the shoulder must be replaced. Before re-fitting the h.t. pick-up, clean the slip-ring track and flanges by pressing a soft, dry cloth on the ring (using a suitably shaped piece of wood) while the engine is turned slowly.

Renewing High-tension Cables. Signs of perishing or cracking in the high-tension cables implies their replacement at once, using 7-mm P.V.C. or Neoprene-covered ignition cable.

To replace a high-tension cable remove the metal washer and moulded terminal from the defective cable; then thread the new cable through the moulded terminal and cut back the insulation for about $\frac{1}{4}$ in. (6·0 mm), pass the exposed strands through the metal washer and bend them back radially. Finally, screw the terminal into the pick-up moulding.

LUCAS A.C./D.C. LIGHTING AND IGNITION
(350 and 500 c.c. models, except T100A, T90 and T100S/S, to Engine No. H 32464, and 650 c.c. models to Engine No. DU 24874)

General Description. Electrical energy in the form of rectified A.C. passes through the battery from the alternator, the rate of charge depending on the position of the lighting switch. During daytime running, the alternator output is sufficient only to supply the ignition coil and to trickle-charge the battery. When the lighting switch is turned to "Pilot" or "Head" ("P" and "H") positions the output increases proportionately.

Under "Emergency" starting conditions, trickle-charging continues while an ignition performance, similar to that from a magneto, is obtained. It is of paramount importance to remember the following: After the engine has been started, normal running is resumed by turning the ignition key from "EMG" to "IGN." If the battery must be removed, the engine can be run with the ignition switch in the "EMG" position, provided that the battery negative cable (brown) is earthed to the frame. Under these conditions no lighting is available.

Circuit Details. The alternator stator carries three pairs of series-connected coils (*see* Figs. 24 and 24a), one pair being permanently connected across the rectifier bridge network. The latter pair provide some degree of charging current for the battery whenever the engine is running.

Connexions to the remaining coil vary according to the positions of the lighting and ignition controls. The alternator output from the battery-charging coils is regulated to the minimum by interaction of the rotor flux set up by the current flowing in the short-circuited coils during daylight running. In the "Pilot" position these latter coils are disconnected and the regulating fluxes are reduced; the alternator output, therefore, increases and compensates for the extra parking-light load. The alternator output is further increased in the "Head" position by the connexion of all three pairs of coils in parallel.

Emergency Starting (Ignition Switch at "EMG"). With this circuit the contact-breaker opens when the alternating current in the windings reaches the maximum. When current flows and the contacts are closed, the main circuit to the alternator is through one arm of the rectifier bridge. At the moment of contact separation, the built-up energy of the alternator windings quickly discharges through an alternative circuit provided by the battery and the ignition coil primary windings; this rapid transfer of energy from alternator to coil causes h.t. current to be induced in the ignition coil secondary winding and a spark to occur at the plug.

Since, when the engine is running and the ignition switch is at "EMG," the battery receives a charging current, soon the battery voltage begins to rise. This voltage opposes the alternator voltage, gradually bringing about a reduction in the energy available to the coil. This reduction in energy, owing to the misfiring which results, will remind the rider to return the ignition key to the "IGN" position.

As previously mentioned, emergency starting with the battery removed necessitates prior earthing of the cable normally connected to the negative terminal of the battery. Do not forget this, and replace the battery as soon as possible to avoid damaging the rectifier.

Construction. The alternator consists of a spigot-mounted and bolted 6-coil laminated stator with the centre-bored rotor carried on, and driven by, an extension to the crankshaft. The rotor has a hexagonal steel core, each face of which carries a high-energy permanent magnet keyed to a laminated pole-tip. The pole tips are riveted to brass side plates, the assembly being cast in aluminium and machined to give a smooth external finish. The stator and rotor can be separated without the need arising to fit magnet keepers to the rotor poles.

The alternator is designed for use with headlamp bulbs not exceeding 30-watts rating.

The Alternator. The alternator requires no attention except for occasional inspection of the snap-connectors in the three green output cables (*see* Fig. 24a). These must be kept clean and tight.

The Lucas Rectifier. The rectifier comprises four plates (coated on one side with selenium) and operates like a non-return valve; it allows current to pass in *one direction* only. The alternating current from the Lucas alternator is thereby converted to unidirectional (d.c.) current for charging the battery.

The rectifier does not require any maintenance except to see that the connexions (*see* Fig. 25) are kept tight and clean, and to check periodically

LIGHTING AND IGNITION SYSTEMS

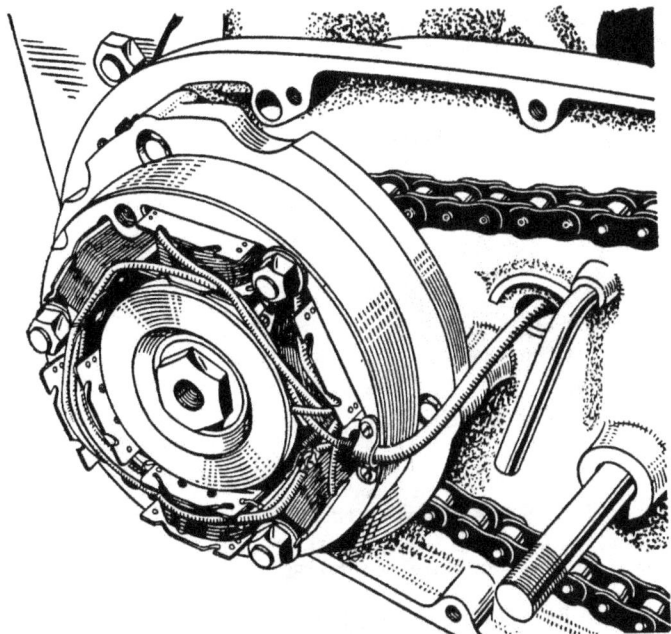

Fig. 24. Primary chain-case cover removed to show rotor and stator

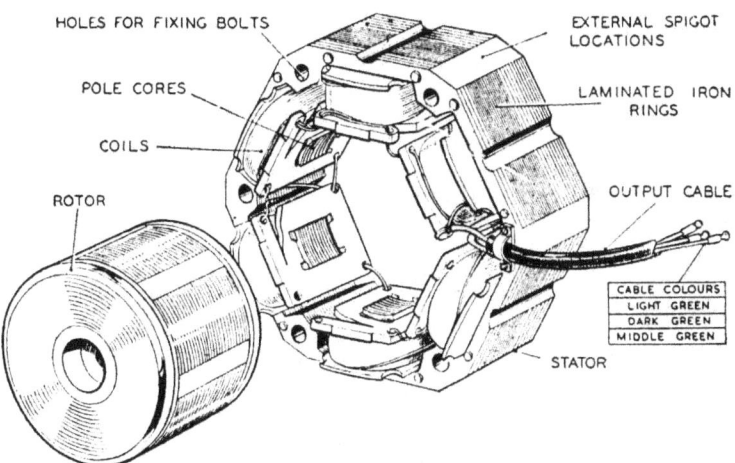

Fig. 24a. Alternator (Model R.M. 14)

that the nut which secures the rectifier to the frame is quite tight. *On no account loosen the nut which clamps the rectifier plates together.* This nut

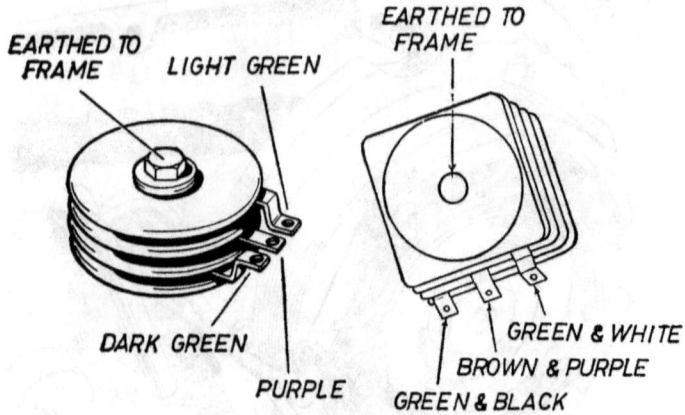

Fig. 25. The Lucas rectifiers showing connexions

The rectifier shown on the left is fitted to 1956–60 models. That on the right is fitted to many 1961–2 models. All 1963–8 models have a small black silicon diode type

is most carefully adjusted during the original assembly of the rectifier. Slackening it can affect the proper functioning of the unit.

The Lucas Battery. This, of course, is concerned with both lighting and ignition. It must be regularly attended to. Battery maintenance is dealt with on pages 61–63.

Ignition Coil. Keep the ignition coil clean, particularly between the terminals, and the lead connexions tight.

Lubrication of Contact-breaker (Distributor DKX2A). Lubricate this unit (*see* Fig. 26) every 5,000 miles. Remove the metal cover and smear the face of the cam lightly with one of the greases recommended for the grease gun on page 39. If this is not available, clean engine oil may be used. On no account must grease be allowed to get on to or near the contacts.

Lubricate the automatic timing-control mechanism, using a thin machine-oil.

Cleaning Distributor DKX2A. Remove the distributor cover every 5,000 miles, and wipe it inside and outside with a clean, dry, fluffless cloth. The contact-breaker should be examined; the contacts should be free from grease or oil. Clean with a fine carborundum stone or very fine emery cloth if burned or blackened, then wipe away any dirt or metal dust with a clean petrol-moistened cloth.

LIGHTING AND IGNITION SYSTEMS

The easiest way to clean the contact-breaker is first to take off the moving contact by unscrewing the nut securing the end of the spring (*see* Fig. 26) and withdrawing the spring washer, spring and bush. Clean the

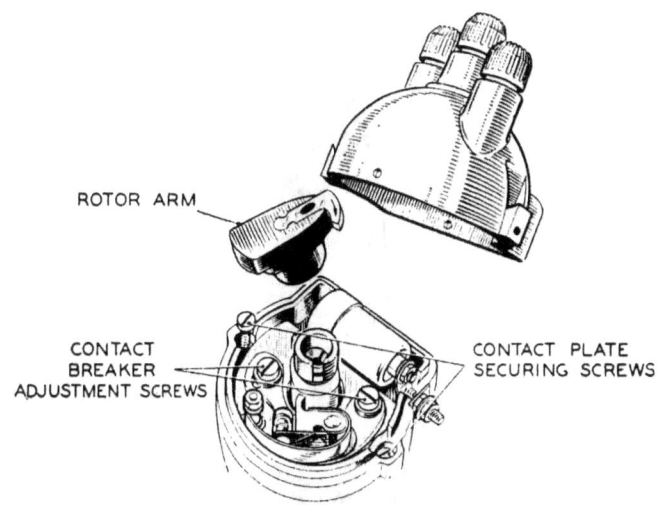

Fig. 26. Distributor (Lucas Model DKX2A with cover removed)

Fitted to most 500 and 650 c.c. pre-unit-construction Triumph Twin engines

pivot pin and smear it very lightly with some clean engine oil prior to replacing the moving-contact arm and its spring.

Contact-breaker Gap (Distributor DKX2A). This should be checked after the first 500 miles and afterwards every 3,000 miles. To check, remove the sparking plugs and turn the engine over slowly until the contacts are fully open, then insert a 0·014 in.–0·016 in. (0·36–0·4 mm) feeler gauge between the contacts. The gauge will be a sliding fit if the gap is correct. Any appreciable variation from the gauge thickness means adjusting the setting. To adjust, if necessary, keep the engine in the position which gives maximum contact opening, and slacken the screw at the side of the body unit; then slide the fixed contact carrier into its slotted hole until the correct gap is obtained. Re-tighten the screw.

Lubrication and Cleaning of Contact-breaker (Distributor 18D2). In the case of machines with a 18D2 distributor, these operations should be attended to about every 6,000 miles. Withdraw and clean the distributor cover inside and outside. Direct special attention to the spaces between the metal electrodes in the cover, and see that the small carbon brush moves freely in its holder.

Lift off the rotor arm (*see* Fig. 27), and unscrew the two screws which secure the contact-breaker base plate. Then remove the base plate and lubricate the automatic ignition-advance mechanism with some clean

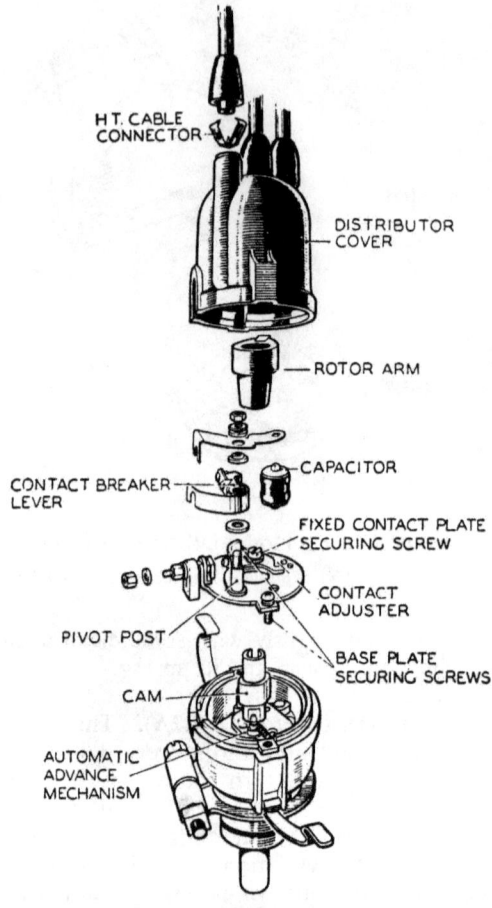

Fig. 27. Distributor (Lucas Model 18D2) shown dismantled

Fitted to most 350, 500 c.c. unit-construction models, except T90 and T100S/S, prior to engine No. H 40528, and and to some pre-unit-construction 650 c.c. models

engine oil; pay special attention to the pivots. Replace the base plate and the rotor arm.

Inspect the contact-breaker closely. Both contacts should be free from oil or grease. If the contacts are blackened or burned, clean them with a slip of fine carborundum stone or with some *very fine* emery cloth. Afterwards with a clean petrol-moistened cloth wipe away any traces of metal

LIGHTING AND IGNITION SYSTEMS 53

dust or dirt. The proper cleaning of the two contacts is much simplified by first removing the contact-breaker lever which carries the moving contact. Lightly smear the cam and pivot post with a little Mobilgrease No. 2 or clean engine oil before replacing the contact-breaker lever. But be most careful not to allow any oil or grease to get on or close to the actual contacts. This is most important. Having cleaned the distributor unit and the contacts, check the gap between the contacts.

Contact-breaker Gap (Distributor 18D2). Check the gap on a new model 3TA or 5TA after covering 500 miles, and subsequently about every 3,000 miles. To check the contact-breaker gap, remove both sparking plugs and turn the engine over slowly until the contacts are seen to be wide open. Then insert a suitable gauge between the contacts. If the gap is correct, the gauge should be a nice sliding fit between them. The correct gap is 0·014 in.–0·016 in.

Where a gap adjustment is called for, keep the engine in the position which causes full opening of the contacts and loosen the screw which secures the fixed contact plate. Insert a screwdriver between the two studs on the base plate and the notch in the fixed contact plate, and adjust the position of the plate until a 0·014 in. gap is obtained between the contacts. Afterwards tighten the securing screw and again check that the gap is correct.

High-tension Cables. Replace the high-tension cables if they show signs of perishing or cracking, using a 7-mm, P.V.C. or Neoprene-covered ignition cable. This is easily done by removing the metal washer and moulded nut from the defective cable. Then thread the new cable through the moulded nut and bare the conductor for about ¼ in. Pass the exposed strands through the metal washer and bend back the strands radially. Finally, re-fit the moulded nut into the h.t. terminal.

LUCAS ENERGY-TRANSFER IGNITION AND BATTERY CHARGING SYSTEM (MODELS T100A, T90 AND T100S/S)

This electrical system has been used on model T100A and in a slightly modified form on models T90 and T100S/S with direct lighting. The distributor/contact-breaker unit for model T100A is shown in Fig. 27 and the contact-breaker for models T90 and T100S/S in Fig. 28.

The energy-transfer (E.T.) ignition system for model T100A includes the basic features of magneto and coil ignition, and consequently enables a Triumph Twin so equipped to be ridden when entirely stripped of the battery and lighting equipment. The system includes a Lucas RM15 alternator (with two windings for ignition, and four for battery charging); a Lucas rectifier; a Lucas battery; a special type of ignition coil; and a Lucas type 18D2 distributor/contact-breaker unit.

The lighting switch automatically regulates the current output from the RM15 alternator via a rectifier, the charge being at its maximum with the switch in the "OFF" position, and at its minimum with the switch in the "H" position.

For routine maintenance instructions, refer to the appropriate sections and paragraphs in this chapter dealing with the various Lucas components comprising the electrical equipment. A special note: with the E.T. ignition system *accurate* ignition timing is *vital* (*see* pages 96 and 127).

LUCAS A.C./D.C. LIGHTING AND IGNITION (350 AND 500 c.c. MODELS FROM ENGINE No. H 32465, AND 650 c.c. MODELS FROM ENGINE No. DU 24875)

General Description. On *all* models a Lucas RM19 alternator, enclosed in the oil-bath chain case, is operated from the crankshaft on its near-side. It supplies current for a single 6-volt battery, two 6-volt batteries (connected in series), or a single 12-volt battery. A silicon diode rectifier converts the a.c. current from the alternator into d.c. current before it reaches the battery used for coil-ignition and lighting (not used for ignition if E.T. ignition is provided).

Battery charging from the alternator is entirely regulated, according to demands, by the lighting and ignition switches positions, but in the case of all 12-volt battery models with a Zener diode (*see* Fig. 30) provided in circuit with the battery, this diode is solely responsible for regulating the current output to the battery according to its state of charge.

The coil-ignition system includes a duplex type 4CA contact-breaker (6CA: 1968–9) driven from the exhaust camshaft, and two ignition coils (one for each cylinder) fed with d.c. current *via* the contact-breaker. Maintenance of all Lucas lighting and ignition equipment is not exacting or complex, but irrespective of what equipment is provided, *always keep all electrical components and connexions, including the earth points to the motor-cycle frame, clean and tight.*

Emergency Starting. Remember that on any model having a 6-volt battery but not provided with a Zenor diode, you can effect a quick start even if the battery is flat by turning the ignition key to the "EMG" position (*see* page 7) so as to enable the d.c. current to by-pass the battery, one contact-breaker, and one ignition coil. After a start in this manner, immediately return the ignition key to the "IGN" position, otherwise the contacts of the contact-breaker may become burned and pitted.

Also remember that on any model having a 12-volt battery and provided with a Zener diode, you can effect a quick start with a flat battery without moving the ignition key from its normal position.

The Contact-breaker Gaps. About every 3,000 miles, and after the first 500 miles, check both contact-breaker gaps with a suitable feeler gauge. The correct gap is 0·014 in.–0·016 in. To obtain access to the contact-breaker, shown in Fig. 28, remove the two screws which secure the circular

LIGHTING AND IGNITION SYSTEMS

chromium-plated cover to the offside of the engine. Rotate the engine with the kickstarter until one pair of contacts is fully open. Then measure the gap and if incorrect loosen the slotted nut which secures the stationary

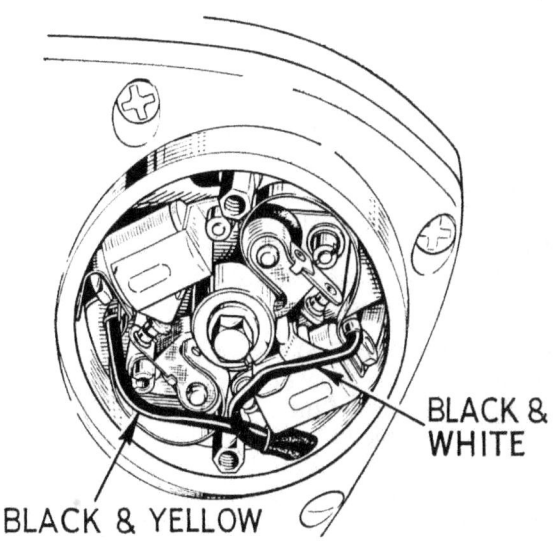

Fig. 28. 4CA Lucas contact-breaker unit pre-1968 (see page 127)

Fitted to all 350 and 500 c.c. unit-construction engines from engine No. H 40528 and to all 650 c.c. unit-construction engines from No. DU 101 onwards. Models T90 and T100S/S also have this design of contact-breaker assembly. L.H. and R.H. leads go to R.H. and L.H. plugs

contact and move the contact until the gap is found to be correct. Afterwards tighten the slotted nut and rotate the engine until the second pair of contacts is fully open. Then adjust their gap in a similar manner.

Cleaning the Contacts (Contact-breaker Type 4CA). Every 3,000 miles when checking the contact-breaker gaps inspect the contacts. If the contacts are burnt or pitted remove them from the base plate and clean them with *very fine* emery cloth. Renew deeply pitted contacts. Afterwards clean, replace the contacts for R.H. cylinder (black and yellow lead); turn engine *forward* until the rocker-arm heel just passes beyond the ramp of the auto-advance cam, giving maximum contact opening; set the gap to 0·015 in. Then turn the engine *forward* through 360° and fit, regap similarly the contacts for the L.H. cylinder.

Place a few drops of thin oil (engine oil is suitable) on the centrifugal automatic-advance mechanism and also one to two drops on the felt pad which lubricates the cam. Apply two drops of oil to the cam support spindle. Be most careful not to allow any oil to get on the contacts.

The Alternator (Type RM19). No attention to the alternator housed in the primary chain case is necessary other than to keep the three snap connectors clean and tight in the output cable below the engine.

The Lighting and Ignition Switches (Type 88SA). Both switches have multi-pin bases and these snap into corresponding sockets in the wiring harness. The pins are spaced irregularly so that the switch can be fitted only in the correct position. The switches are sealed and if you suspect a fault, test by substituting another switch.

There is no "EMG" position on the 88SA type ignition switch fitted to most 350 and 500 c.c. models with a nacelle and also fitted to earlier 650 c.c. model 6T with a nacelle. On the later version of model 6T (engine No. DU 24875 onwards), however, the ignition switch has an "EMG" position but because of the wiring circuit provided, it is *not* operative and the engine can be started up with the ignition key in the normal starting position irrespective of battery condition.

The Ignition Switch (Type S45). Most 350, 500 and 650 c.c. models without a nacelle have the type of switch incorporated with the L/H switch panel. As in the case of the 88SA switch, it has no "EMG" position and its design is of the "barrel" type requiring *one* specific "Yale" key to operate it. Keep available the details of the correct key number to ensure correct replacement in the event of your losing the ignition key.

On Triumph Twins without a nacelle and fitted with an S45 type ignition switch, a cut-out button is fitted as indicated on page 2, and an ignition warning light (red) is incorporated in the shell of the Lucas headlamp. This warning light remains on, with the engine running or stopped, until the ignition is switched off. To prevent battery discharge *via* the contact-breaker, *always switch off the ignition after stopping the engine with the cut-out button.*

The Rectifier (Type 2DS506). This type of silicon-diode rectifier is fitted to all 350, 500 and 650 c.c. models to convert a.c. current to d.c.

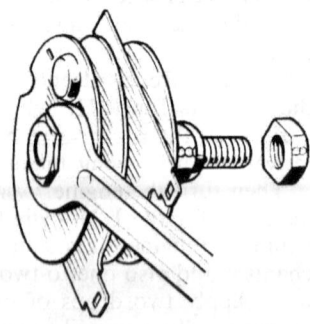

Fig. 29. Correct spanner application when securing rectifier to frame

LIGHTING AND IGNITION SYSTEMS 57

current. Note the remarks on page 48. It is essential that the central fixing bolt of the rectifier always makes good electrical contact with the motor-cycle frame, and that the self-locking nut which clamps the rectifier plates together is never disturbed. Should the plates become twisted, the internal connexions will be broken and the rectifier fail.

When securing a rectifier firmly to the frame of the motor-cycle, hold the spanners as indicated in Fig. 29. Note that the securing bolt and nut both have $\frac{1}{4}$ × 28 U.N.F. threads, and have identification circles.

The Zener Diode (Model ZD715). On 350, 500, 650 c.c. models with 12-volt battery equipment this small, curious-looking device, mounted

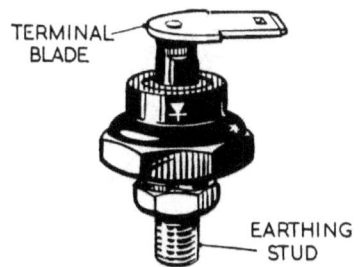

Fig. 30. Rather odd-looking but very functional—the Zener diode (Model ZD715)

Provided on all Triumph Twins with 12-volt electrics. Prior to 1968 the flat aluminium heat-sink plate for the Zener diode was housed in the space behind the hinged side-panel carrying the ignition and lighting switches. From 1968 onwards the Zener diode unit has been transferred to a cone-shaped finned casting mounted beneath the Lucas headlamp

on a "heat sink" plate to obtain efficient cooling, regulates battery charging.

No maintenance of the Zener diode is necessary other than to keep the diode and aluminium "sink" absolutely clean and dry. The flow of air around the latter must not be impaired in any way. Do not use a mop and water to clean the "sink"! Referring to Fig. 30, be careful never to tighten the earthing stud excessively. The diode body is made of copper and the earthing stud has a low-tensile strength.

The Ignition Coils (Types MA6, MA12). The twin coils are rubber-mounted to the motor-cycle frame below the petrol tank. Keep the top of each coil clean, especially between the terminals. Occasionally inspect the cables for frayed wires or damaged insulation. Replace any damaged section of the cable.

Battery Maintenance. All batteries used for dynamo lighting, or coil ignition and electric lighting, are of the Lucas lead-acid type. For appropriate maintenance instructions, *see* pages 61–63.

The Live Fuse. A 35 ampere-rating live fuse is included in the battery-to-earth lead of the electrical circuit. It is enclosed in a quickly detachable plastic tube holder and secured by a quickly-detachable cap with bayonet fixing.

Should you wish at any time to add any additional electrical equipment to your Triumph, it may be necessary to increase the fuse rating. If the engine begins to behave rather erratically, it is advisable to check that the live fuse has not "blown" before making further detailed investigations.

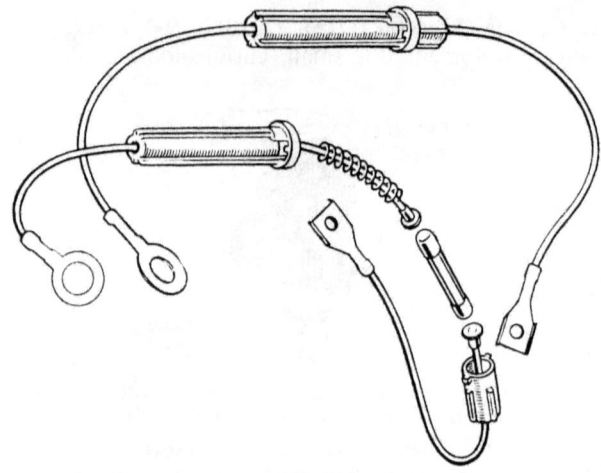

Fig. 31. Exploded view of fuse cartridge and holder assembly

(*From Triumph Workshop Manual*)

This check can save much time and trouble. Always fit a new fuse cartridge (*see* Fig. 31) if you have any suspicion about the condition of the existing fuse on your mount.

LUCAS LAMPS (1956-69 MODELS)

Headlamps. All Lucas headlamps fitted to 1956 and later Triumph Twins are of the "pre-focus" type which require no focusing adjustment but some vertical beam-setting, when necessary, in order to give maximum illumination without causing dazzle to other road users. Their design varies to some extent, mainly according to whether a nacelle is included or not. If a nacelle is not provided, the headlamp is mounted between brackets integral with the telescopic front forks.

Correct Headlamp Bulbs to Fit. Each Lucas headlamp requires a double-filament main bulb, and a single-filament pilot bulb which is a push-fit in the rear of the light-unit comprising the lens and reflector which are sealed and non-detachable. The holder for the main bulb is

LIGHTING AND IGNITION SYSTEMS

also secured to the rear of the light-unit. Always renew "blown" bulbs with *genuine* Lucas bulbs of the correct type which are as follows—

The Main Bulb. On all 1956-69 pre-unit-construction and unit-construction models having 6-volt electrical equipment, except 650 c.c. Triumph "Trophy" and "Bonneville" models, the correct main bulb for the headlamp is a pre-focus, double-filament, 6-volt 30/24-watt Lucas No. 373 (L.H. dip). In the case of the above-named 650 c.c. models the correct replacement bulb is a pre-focus, double-filament, 6-volt, 30/24-watt Lucas No. 312 (vertical dip).

The correct main bulb to fit to the headlamp of all 1963 and later 650 c.c. models having 12-volt electrical equipment is a 12-volt, 50/40-watt Lucas No. 414 (L.H. dip).

The Pilot Bulb. For all 1956 and later Triumph Twin models provided with 6-volt electrical equipment the correct replacement pilot bulb is a 6-volt, 3-watt Lucas No. 988 M.C.C. bulb. For 1963 and subsequent models having 12-volt electrical equipment the correct bulb to use is a 12-volt, 4-watt Lucas No. 222 M.C.C.

Replacing the Headlamp Bulb (Nacelle Fitted). Access to the headlamp bulb is gained by slackening the front rim retaining screw located at the top of the nacelle cover. Disengage and withdraw the front rim and light-unit assembly, first removing the upper edge. Press the moulded adaptor inwards and turn it to the left. Lift off the adaptor and withdraw the bulb. When fitting the replacement bulb, locate the slot in the bulb flange with the projection in the bulb holder; re-fit the adaptor, engaging its three projections with the corresponding slots in the bulb holder, then press inwards and secure by turning the adaptor to the right.

After fitting a new main bulb (*see* Fig. 32) replace the light-unit and rim assembly to the nacelle, locating the bottom edge of the rim first. Finally tighten the screw which secures the rim in place and check the beam setting. Many garages to-day have a Lucas beamsetter which enables the headlamp beam to be quickly and accurately set. If this equipment is not available locally, attend to beam setting as described in a later paragraph.

Replacing the Headlamp Bulb (No Nacelle). Where the headlamp is mounted between brackets integral with the telescopic front forks, the above procedure is also applicable, but the screw securing the rim is, of course, fitted to the top of the headlamp instead of the nacelle.

Before fitting a new main or pilot bulb to the headlamp, always make quite sure that its type No., voltage and wattage (*see* above) are correct.

Renewing Pilot Bulb (All Models). Remove the front rim and light-unit assembly as previously described and pull the pilot-bulb holder (*see* Fig. 32) from the rear of the reflector. Renew the dud bulb, fit a new one to the holder, and push the latter back into the reflector.

Setting the Headlamp Beam. Place the machine in front of a light coloured wall at a distance of about 25 feet when setting the headlamp beam. During this check, the motor-cycle should be carrying its normal load, as the rider's weight (and that of a pillion passenger) is liable to affect the setting. Switch on the main beam, directing this straight ahead

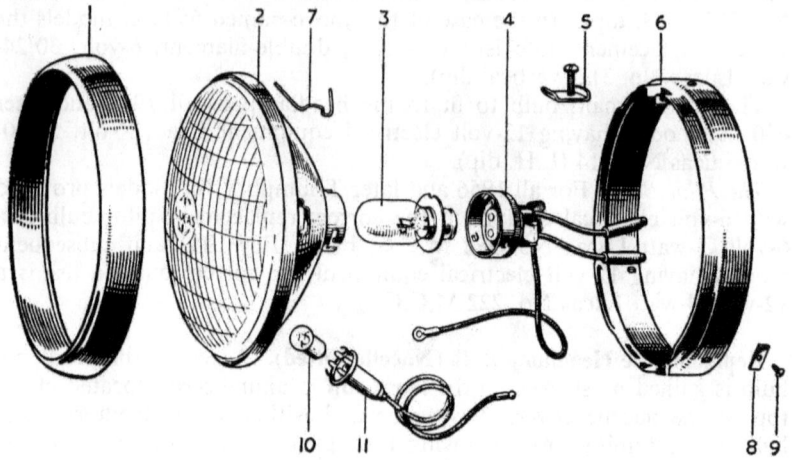

Fig. 32. Showing details of Lucas pre-focus headlamp

The exploded view shown applies to 1956–67 models; where a nacelle is not fitted a headlamp shell replaces item No. 6. 1968-9 models have separate headlamps

1. Front rim
2. The light-unit
3. Pre-focus main bulb
4. Main bulb adaptor
5. Plate securing 1
6. Lamp fixing ring (nacelle models only)
7. Wire clip
8. Tapped plate
9. Screw for 8
10. 6-W pilot bulb
11. Pilot-bulb holder

and parallel with the ground. If this direction is not obtained, loosen the two small screws on each side of the lamp fixing ring and raise or lower the beam by pulling-out or pressing-in the bottom of the ring until the beam is focused at about 2 feet, 6 inches from the base of the wall. On some "Trophy" models (without nacelle headlamp) to adjust the beam, slacken the two headlamp securing bolts and tilt the headlamp as required. When the required beam has been obtained, re-tighten the two screws.

The Stop-tail Lamp. To renew the double-filament bulb, remove the two slotted screws securing the plastic lens and withdraw the latter from the lamp body, followed by the double-filament bulb from the bulb holder. The correct replacement for the stop-tail lamp is a Lucas No. 384 6-volt 6/18-watt bulb. This bulb has offset securing pins to prevent incorrect insertion into the bulb holder and to ensure that the higher wattage filament is illuminated when the brake pedal is depressed. Should the 6-watt filament fail, do not change the cables over to obtain rear lighting from the 18-watt filament as the heat generated is liable to burn the plastics lens.

LUCAS BATTERY MAINTENANCE

All Lucas batteries fitted to 1956–69 models (usually below the hinged dualseat) are of the lead-acid type. That fitted to most 1956-9 Triumph Twins is the Lucas 6-volt PU7E/9 type shown in Fig. 33. Later models with 6-volt equipment have a Lucas 6-volt type ML9E, MLZ9E, MK9E, or MKZ9E battery. On later unit-construction models with a.c./d.c. lighting and ignition, and a Zener diode to control battery charging, however, a single 12-volt battery (type PUZ5A) is provided, or alternatively two 6-volt batteries of the above-mentioned "M" type are connected in series to give 12 volts. All Lucas batteries except the PU7E/9 type have moulded cases in translucent polystyrene, thereby enabling the level of the electrolyte to be visible from outside the battery.

Topping-up. The electrolyte (acid solution) level in the cells of the battery must be maintained, so once a week (monthly on the Lucas

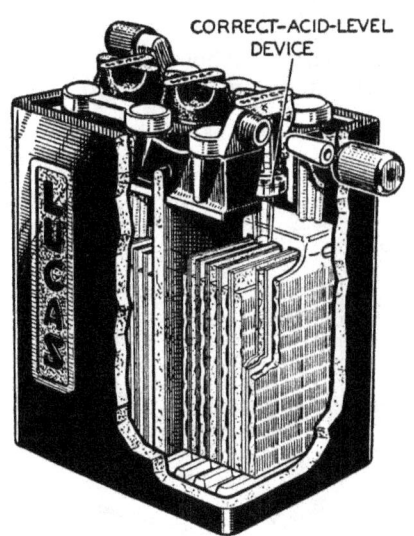

Fig. 33. Lucas battery model PU7E/9

Showing correct-acid-level device and detachable cable connectors. This battery is fitted to many 1956–59 models

PU7E/9 type) this should be examined. If required, *distilled* water must be added to bring the electrolyte level correct in each cell.

A naked light must not be used when examining the condition of the cells, as there is a risk of igniting the gas coming from the active materials.

The correct acid-solution-level device on the PU7E/9 battery consists of a central tube with a perforated flange which rests on a ledge in the filling orifice (*see* Fig. 33). When topping-up a battery fitted with this device, pour distilled water around the flange (not down the tube) until no more drains through into the cell. This happens when the electrolyte level reaches the bottom of the central tube and so prevents further escape of the air displaced by topping-up with water. If the tube is then lifted slightly, the small amount of water in the flange will drain into the cell and the acid solution level will be correct.

Note that the Lucas ML9E, MLZ9E, MK9E and MKZ9E batteries with translucent casings must not be topped up to the top of the separators. The correct filling line is moulded in the casing as may be seen in Fig. 34. The battery must be lifted out of its carrier and distilled water added until the liquid reaches the coloured "maximum acid level" line.

Where a Lucas 6-volt type PU7E/9 or 12-volt type PUZ5A battery is fitted, the electrolyte in each cell should be topped-up until it is just level with the top of the plate separators or just above the plates respectively. Note that only in the case of the two batteries specified above is it possible to use a hydrometer to check the specific gravity of the electrolyte (1·280–1·300, battery fully charged).

Other Battery Maintenance. About every 1,000 miles or monthly (more often in hot climates) remove the cover from the battery and

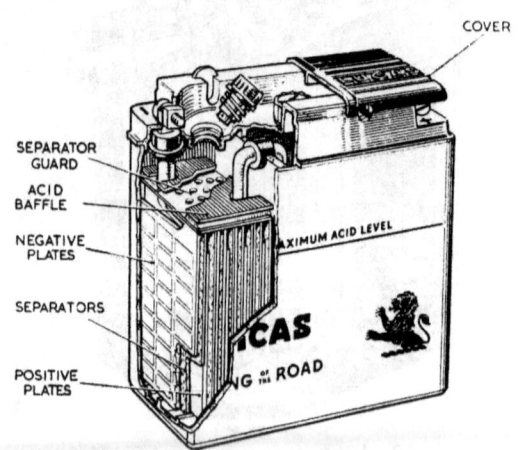

Fig. 34. The Lucas ML9E or MLZ9E battery

thoroughly clean the top of the latter. Also inspect the battery terminals and if found corroded, scrape them clean and smear with some petroleum jelly. Remove all vent plugs, check that their vent holes are unobstructed, and that their washers are in sound condition. Renew the rubber washers if necessary.

LIGHTING AND IGNITION SYSTEMS   63

The battery must not be left in a discharged condition. Should the machine be out of use for any length of time, have the battery fully charged and every two weeks have it given a short refreshing charge, so as to prevent any likelihood of the plates becoming permanently sulphated.

Battery Connexions. The red positive (+) terminal of the battery *on all models must be earthed* to the frame of the motor-cycle (*via* a 35 ampere line-fuse on machines with 12-volt equipment). Accidental earthing of the battery negative (−) terminal can cause serious damage.

If a 650 c.c. model has two 6-volt batteries, the main harness feed wire must be connected to the negative terminal of one of the two batteries. The positive terminal of this battery must also be connected to the negative terminal of the second battery, the remaining positive wire being earthed to the frame *via* a 35 ampere line-fuse.

Detachable Cable Connectors. When connecting the battery, unscrew the knurled nut and withdraw the collet or cone-shaped insert. Remember this is not interchangeable with the collet in the other terminal. Bare the end of the cable about one inch and thread one bared end through the knurled nut and collet; then bend back the cable strands over the narrow end of the collet and insert the collet and cable into the terminal block. Tighten the knurled nut to secure the connexion.

Wiring Diagrams for Lucas Electrical Equipment. Many different wiring diagrams (for which space is not available in this handbook) cover all Lucas equipment specified on 1956–69 350, 500 and 650 c.c. pre-unit construction and unit-construction Triumph Twins. Provided that you maintain the equipment properly and do not allow the wiring harness and its leads to become chafed, you are unlikely to have to refer to the appropriate complex wiring diagram.

Wiring diagrams are included in all Triumph Instruction Manuals, Owner's Handbooks and Workshop Manuals and can be referred to, when necessary, in one of these publications obtainable from Triumph dealers or from the Triumph Engineering Co. Ltd. (*see* page 120). Note that separate wiring diagrams can in most cases be obtained by contacting Joseph Lucas Ltd., Great Hampton Street, Birmingham, 18. It is advisable to mention full details (including date of manufacture, model and its engine number) of your Triumph to ensure prompt attention and the supplying of the correct wiring diagram.

THE HORN

The electric horns fitted to Triumph motor-cycles are adjusted to give their best performance before being passed out of the works; they give a long period of service without attention.

Should the action of the horn become uncertain—emitting a choking sound only—it is not proof that it has broken down. It is possible the trouble is due to some outside source—a discharged battery, a loose connexion, or short-circuit in the wiring of the horn, or the horn-push bracket may not be in good electrical contact with the handlebars. Check these possible sources of trouble, especially if the horn functions very badly or ceases to operate. If everything is found to be O.K., adjust the horn for possible wear of some of its internal moving parts. When adjusting and testing the horn do not depress the horn push for more than a fraction of a second, otherwise the wiring circuit may become overloaded.

To make a horn adjustment, turn the small serrated adjustment screw (located near its terminals) *anti-clockwise* until the horn ceases to sound.

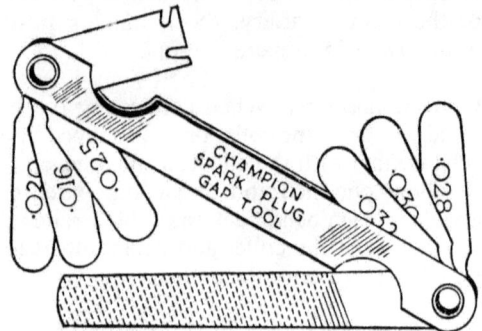

Fig. 35. An extremely useful Champion tool

This sparking plug maintenance tool has, as may be observed, a slotted blade for adjusting the earth electrode(s), six feeler gauges for checking the plug gap, and a fine file for cleaning off glazed electrode deposits and squaring off parallel surfaces

Then turn the screw *clockwise* about one-quarter to one-half turn as required. If the horn still remains dumb or sounds peculiar, have it examined by a specialist at a Lucas Service Depot.

SPARKING PLUGS

Suitable Sparking Plugs. Always run on a sparking plug suitable for the particular machine concerned, and recommended by the engine manufacturers. Three very reliable types of sparking plugs are the Lodge, the K.L.G., and the Champion. Waterproof terminal covers and watertight plugs corresponding to the standard types are also available if desired.

Engines with light-alloy or cast-iron cylinder heads require 14 mm plugs with $\frac{3}{4}$ in. or $\frac{1}{2}$ in. reach respectively. Never use long-reach plugs for short-reach ones. Suitable $\frac{3}{4}$ in. reach plugs for touring and general use are the Champion N4, the Lodge HLN and the K.L.G. FE–75. All the above are 14 mm. plugs. Suitable 14 mm. sparking plugs with a $\frac{1}{2}$ in. reach are the Champion L7, the Lodge HN and the K.L.G. F–75.

Another make of sparking plug popular in the U.K. and elsewhere, and used by the winners of 1967 500, 350, 250, 125 c.c. T.T. races is the

LIGHTING AND IGNITION SYSTEMS 65

non-detachable NGK. This plug differs from the others in that the upper part of its central electrode is made of copper. It is, like the three other makes referred to, obtainable from most large accessory firms and garages.

For Triumph Twins the following NGK types are suitable: for models T100 and T110 (cast-iron cylinder heads)—B-8H or B-77HC; for models

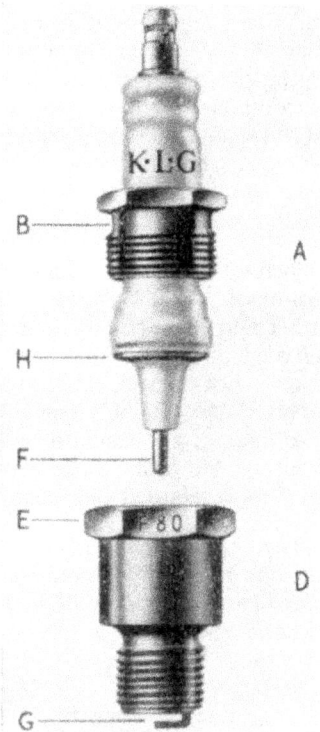

Fig. 36. Detachable-type sparking plug (K.L.G.) dismantled for thorough cleaning

The gland nut B and the internal washer H are shown still in position on the insulation

T110 (alloy head), T100S/S, T120 and TR6S/S—B-8E or B-77EC; for models 5T, 5TA, T90 and T100 (alloy head), T100A, TR5 and TR6—B-7E or B-7EC; for models 3TA and 6T—B-7H or B-7HC. Plug types having the letter "C" at the end are competition plugs, but these plugs are also suitable for touring purposes. They can be subjected to greater engine r.p.m. and heat than the standard-type. Both types are most reliable.

Correct Sparking Plug Gap. Difficult starting or occasional misfiring can usually be traced to a dirty or unserviceable sparking plug. The life of a good plug is considerable, but the points of the electrodes gradually burn away and eventually the gap becomes too large and it is necessary to reset the points.

It is advisable to check the plug gap regularly (say every 3,000 miles) and to adjust the gap on both sparking plugs if burning of the points has caused the gap to exceed the maximum correct gap. The makers of Triumphs recommend a gap of 0·018 in.–0·020 in. Check the gap with a suitable feeler gauge. The gauge should just enter without springing the points.

When adjusting the plug gap, never attempt to bend or tap the *centre* electrode. Use a pair of snipe-nose pliers, or a plug re-gapping tool (shown in Fig. 35), to bend the outside (earth) electrode(s). Tapping the earth electrode(s) is not a good method. When the plug has to be thoroughly cleaned, this should be done as described below, and the plug re-gapped *afterwards*.

Plug Examination. When a plug has been removed the condition of the insulator should be examined. If it is *light brown*, it shows that the mixture strength is correct and that the engine is running at the correct temperature; if it is *dull black*, it proves that the plug is running too cold and, therefore, the carbon is not burned, this being the result of running on a too-rich mixture or of the engine's being left running with too liberal a slow-running setting; if the insulator is *ash white*, it indicates that the plug is over-heating, the usual cause being that the mixture is too weak or that the ignition is retarded too much.

Cleaning a Sparking Plug. If carburation is correct and excessive oil is not entering the combustion chamber, it should not be necessary to clean, or get cleaned, sparking plugs thoroughly more often than once about every 3,000 miles. When running-in a new or rebored engine, it is advisable to remove and check the plugs for cleanliness at intervals of about 500 miles.

Quick cleaning of a plug can be done by brushing the points and slightly rubbing their firing sides with smooth glass-paper. Alternatively the plug can be cleaned with a proprietary gadget. Thorough cleaning (internal and external), however, is not possible in this manner.

To Clean K.L.G. and Lodge Plugs yourself. Fig. 36 shows a typical detachable type (K.L.G.) sparking plug dismantled for thorough cleaning. To dismantle a detachable-type sparking plug, hold the larger hexagon of the plug body (*D*) lightly in a vice or with a suitable spanner. If you use a vice, be most careful not to exert any pressure on the hexagon faces. Then with a suitable box spanner applied to the smaller hexagon (*B*) of the gland nut, unscrew it until it is separated from the body (*D*)*. The

---

* Where a detachable-type sparking plug has been in service for a very considerable time, the plug may be found extremely difficult to dismantle, in which case the attempt should be abandoned.

LIGHTING AND IGNITION SYSTEMS 67

centre electrode (F) with its insulation (comprising the insulated electrode assembly (A)) can now be detached from the gland nut. Take care not to lose the internal sealing washer (H).

To clean the insulation, wipe it clean with a cloth soaked in petrol or paraffin. If the insulation is coated with hard carbon deposits, remove these with some fine glass paper, but make no attempt to scrape off the deposits. The internal sealing washer (H) and the surfaces on the insulator, and in the metal body on which this washer rests, are very important as they prevent gas leakage through the plug. Therefore wipe them only with a rag soaked in petrol or paraffin. Any damage caused while dismantling will render the plug unserviceable.

To clean the metal parts (plug body and gland nut) wipe them clean with petrol, or, if necessary, scrape off the deposits with a small knife, or use a wire brush. Afterwards rinse the parts in petrol. The gland nut seldom gets very fouled, but the inside of the plug body may be very dirty, and the same may apply to the external threads of the plug. Clean and polish the points of the centre and outside (earth) electrodes shown in Fig. 36 at (F) and (G) with some fine glass paper.

See that there is no dirt or grit lodged between the body of the plug and the insulation, and particularly on the internal sealing washer and the contacting faces. Smear a little thin oil on the internal washer and make sure that it seats properly. When assembling the sparking plug, see that the centre electrode and insulation are positioned centrally in the body bore. If they are not, remove, re-position by rotating assembly (A) a quarter of a turn, and assemble. Do not attempt to force it into position or bend it.

Avoid excessive tightening of the gland nut (B). Finally verify that the plug gap is correct (*see* page 66).

Cleaning with a Service Unit. To clean a plug quickly and well, take it to the nearest garage equipped with a suitable Service Unit. With this apparatus the plug can be cleaned of all deposits in a few minutes, washed, subjected to a high-pressure air line, and afterwards tested for sparking on the garage apparatus at an air pressure of over 100 lb per sq in. Detachable and non-detachable plugs can be similarly dealt with.

Replacing the Plug. Before replacing a plug, renew the steel washer if it is worn or flattened, and clean the plug threads with a wire brush. Screw the plug home by hand as far as possible, and always use the plug spanner for final tightening.

When replacing a sparking plug on a light-alloy cylinder head, smear the threads with graphite and do not over-tighten or difficulty may be experienced in removing the plug after carbon has been deposited around the threads. Renew both plugs about every 10,000 miles.

5 General Maintenance: The Motor-cycle

ADJUSTMENT, lubrication and cleaning of the motor-cycle parts are essential to the smooth running of the machine as a whole. For advice on lubrication and the lighting system, *see* Chapters 3 and 4.

CLEANING

Cleanliness is Important. Keep your mount nice and clean. Doubtless it cost quite a sum, and it is well worth careful looking after. With regular and proper cleaning it will function better, will last longer, maintain its good looks, and retain a good market value. A dirty motor-cycle is an eyesore, and remember that dirt hides defects, encourages rusting, and is a menace when stripping down. Never leave your Triumph Twin soaking wet overnight. If you have no time for cleaning in wet weather, grease the machine all over *before* use. For dirty hands "Swarfega" is excellent.

Cleaning the Engine and Gearbox. See that the cylinder barrel and cylinder-head fins are kept clean and black (except aluminium-alloy heads). If the enamel has worn away, paint the fins with some proprietary cylinder black after thorough cleaning with a stiff brush dipped in paraffin. Note that rusted fins, besides looking shabby, cause an appreciable loss in heat dispersion.

Scour off all filth from the lower part of the engine and gearbox with stiff brushes and paraffin. Clean all aluminium alloy and bright surfaces first with a rag damped in paraffin, assisted by brushes where necessary, and then with a dry rag.

Cleaning the Enamel. Never attempt to remove mud from the enamelled parts when dry and caked, as this is likely to damage the surfaces. Soak the mud off with a hose if available. In the case of a very dirty machine it may be advisable to paint the surfaces over with a cleaning compound such as "Gunk" before directing a stream of water on to the dirty surfaces. Be careful not to allow any water to get on the wheel-hub bearings and a magneto or distributor and coil, and carburettor. If a hose is not available, soak the mud and then disperse it with plenty of clean water, using a sponge and pail. Tar spots can be removed with turpentine.

GENERAL MAINTENANCE: THE MOTOR-CYCLE 69

Having removed all dirt, dry the enamelled surfaces with a chamois leather and afterwards polish them with soft dusters and some good wax polish or a proprietary polish such as "Karpol" or "Autobrite."

"Dry weather" riders can keep a machine in almost showroom condition merely be rubbing the enamel over with a paraffin-damped rag, followed by a dry, soft duster.

Cleaning the Chromium. Never employ liquid metal polish or paste as, this will wear down the thin surface. A good chromium-cleaning compound such as "Belco" can, however, safely be used, though not too frequently. The normal method of removing tarnish (salt deposits) is to clean the surfaces regularly with a damp chamois leather and then polish them with soft dusters.

To Reduce Tarnishing. During the winter months it is a good plan to wipe over occasionally all chromium surfaces with a soft cloth soaked in a proprietary anti-tarnish preparation. An example is "Tekall," obtainable in ½-pint and 1-pint tins.

FORKS AND STEERING HEAD

Maintenance of Triumph Telescopic Front Forks. To ensure smooth and efficient action of the hydraulically-damped front forks, the only maintenance required by you is to: (*a*) check occasionally that *all* external nuts and screws are tight; (*b*) about every 6,000 miles change the damping oil in each fork leg. Should substantial leakage occur, however, change the oil earlier. The oil recommended by the makers is that advised for engine lubrication (*see* page 26), and no topping-up is normally advisable or necessary.

At intervals of approximately 20,000 miles a complete overhaul of the front forks is generally necessary, and this work is best undertaken by the Triumph Service Department or by an established Triumph dealer (*see* Preface).

Draining and Replenishing Fork Legs (1956–57). Drain both legs. Referring to Fig. 37, remove the sloping drain plug (*2*) and washer (*1*) from the outside of the fork leg bottom cover-tube (*7*), just above the wheel spindle, and allow all oil to drain off into a suitable receptacle. To facilitate quick draining of the last drops of oil, operate the forks up and down quickly and firmly by means of the handlebars. When all oil has been drained off from both fork legs, replace and firmly tighten the drain plugs, not omitting the fibre washers.

On nacelle-equipped models to replenish the fork legs it is necessary to remove the headlamp rim and light-unit assembly (*see* page 59) from the nacelle so as to expose the two screwed filler-plugs, one from each fork leg. Remove these from the stanchion and with an oil pressure can or gun, inject ¼ pint (150 c.c.) of suitable engine oil. Note that in the case of

650 c.c. unit-construction models after engine No. DU 5825, and 350 and 500 c.c. models from engine No. H 32465 the engine oil replenishment necessary is ⅓ pint. For 1968–9 fork details. *See* page 130.

On models having the Lucas headlamp mounted between brackets integral with the front forks, and provided with no nacelle, oil replenishment can, of course, be effected from the upper ends of the fork legs after removing the two large chromium-plated nuts.

Checking for Steering Head Play. Check for play every 6,000 miles.*
When adjusting the steering head bearings it is advisable to support the

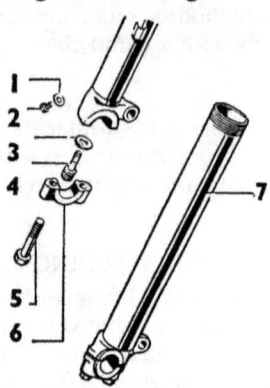

Fig. 37. The bottom end of each front fork leg (1956–67)

1. Washer
2. Drain plug
3. Aluminium washer
4. Cone and dust cover
5. One of 2 bolts for securing 6
6. Wheel-spindle cap
7. Bottom tube cover (L.H.)

machine on the Triumph central stand and also on a box placed underneath the crankcase, so as to relieve the races of all external influence. To test for play in the steering head, slacken off the steering damper, and stand at the nearside of the motor-cycle. Rest the fingers of the right hand on the top steering-head race dust cover and with the left hand raise and lower the nose of the front mudguard (*see* Fig. 38). Any slackness calls for an immediate adjustment. It is assumed, of course, that there is no slackness in the front mudguard.

An alternative method (an easier one) of checking for steering-head play is to stand beside the off-side of your mount with the fingers of your left hand reaching down behind the nacelle (where fitted) and resting on the frame and the dust cover of the steering-head top bearing; with your right hand apply the front brake and rock your Triumph slightly backwards and forwards. With the fingers of your left hand you will then be able to feel any steering-head play which may exist and require removal.

* When running-in a new or reconditioned engine, check for play after covering 500 miles.

GENERAL MAINTENANCE: THE MOTOR-CYCLE 71

To Remove Steering-head Play. This *must* be done with the motor-cycle on its central stand, also preferably with a box placed beneath the engine crankcase to raise the front wheel well clear of the ground. Remove

Fig. 38. One method of checking for steering-head play

This, and an alternative method, are described in the text

the steering-damper knob and slacken the pinch-bolt at the back of the fork top-lug.

Then tighten down the large sleeve adjuster-nut on the fork stem until all steering-head play is *just* removed. By swinging the front forks to the left and right alternately, a suitable spanner can readily be used for turning the nut *clockwise* as required. Be careful not to over-tighten the nut. When making the adjustment, use only two-finger pressure to tighten or loosen it. With the steering-head bearings correctly adjusted, the front forks and wheel should be able, under their own weight, to turn freely from lock to lock without any stiffness or dragging. Should fork movement be jerky or rough in spite of a most careful adjustment having been made, suspect damaged balls and/or bearing races at one or both steering-head bearings. The only remedy in this case is to renew the faulty parts and the appropriate Triumph Workshop Manual should be consulted for correct procedure. Alternatively have the work done by an authorized Triumph dealer or by the Triumph Service Department.

After removing any existing steering-head play, tighten firmly the pinch-bolt at the back of the fork top-lug, replace the steering-damper knob, and finally give the machine a brief road test.

WHEELS, BRAKES, TYRES

Removing the Front Wheel (1956-67 Models). Withdraw the split pin and pivot pin, or clevis from the lower end of the brake cable. On the earlier models TR6, T100 and T110 unscrew the nut and remove the bolt which secures the anchor plate to the fork leg. Remove the two bolts which secure each wheel-spindle cap (6, Fig. 37) to the corresponding bottom tube cover on the fork leg. Slacken the retaining nut at the rear, of the mudguard and swing the front stand forward. Then withdraw the front wheel from the telescopic forks. If necessary, facilitate its removal by exerting pressure on the rear of the motor-cycle.

Fitting the Front Wheel (1956-67 Models). Position the front wheel in the telescopic forks and swing the front stand backwards. If handy, add a small weight in front of the parcel grid on the petrol tank to ensure that the fork legs rest on the wheel spindle. Hold the wheel-spindle caps ((6), Fig. 37) in position and screw the cap-securing bolts a few turns into the front fork bottom tube covers ((7), Fig. 37). Note that the wheel spindle is recessed at the bolt positions and it may prove necessary to move the front wheel slightly from side to side before it is possible to insert the four cap-securing bolts. At this stage do not fully tighten the four bolts.

On models with full-width silver-painted hubs see that the anchor peg on the off-side fork leg engages with the channel on the brake anchor plate. On the earlier TR6, T100 and T110 models insert the brake anchor bolt and tighten it securely. Bounce forks *before* tightening end-cap bolts.

Tighten the four spindle cap-securing bolts ((5), Fig. 37) evenly; keep the space between each cap and fork leg equal in front of and behind the wheel spindle. Refit the front brake cable to the abutment and insert the pivot pin and split pin. Check that the handlebar adjustment for the front brake is correct (*see* page 76). With the front stand in its normal position tighten the securing nut.

Centralizing Brake Shoes. On *all* models loosen the nut on the front brake fulcrum-pin and apply strong pressure with the handlebar lever. Keep this pressure on the lever while tightening the fulcrum-pin nut. The two brake shoes should then be properly synchronized.

GENERAL MAINTENANCE: THE MOTOR-CYCLE 73

The Rear Wheel (Spring Frame Models). The Triumph rear wheel is mounted on journal ball bearings and these bearings have no adjustment. Only after a very big mileage is it necessary to check for bearing slackness. Slackness can be easily checked by placing the motor-cycle on its central stand and testing for lateral movement of the rear wheel. If the bearings are in good shape a negligible amount of lateral movement should be detected. Note that the quickly-detachable wheel on some 350 and 500 c.c. models (after engine No. H 32415) have adjustable taper-roller bearings. The adjustment is provided on the offside of the hub, the inner nut being the adjuster and the outer one the lock-nut. With this type of wheel there should be a minimum of $\frac{1}{64}$ in. side play measured at the rim.

There are two basic types of rear wheels fitted to 1956 and later Triumph Twins: (a) the *standard* type having the brake drum and sprocket secured by eight bolts to the rear hub, and (b) the *quickly-detachable* (Q.D.) type where the wheel-hub is splined to the brake drum and sprocket and can therefore be quickly detached, leaving the chain-guard, the secondary chain, brake drum and sprocket in position on the motor-cycle.

Bearing renewal becomes necessary only after a *very* big mileage and requires considerable skill. You should carefully study the technical advice given in the appropriate Triumph Workshop Manual or, preferably, have the work done by the Triumph Service Department or by an established Triumph dealer.

Removing Standard Rear Wheel (All 1956–69 Spring Frame Models). Follow this procedure. First engage a gear to prevent the secondary chain rotating on the gearbox sprocket, and falling off when the chain spring-link is removed. Remove the spring link and withdraw the secondary chain from the sprocket. Disconnect the rear brake torque stay by removing the rear nut and loosening the front nut and bolt. Unscrew the brake adjuster nut and remove the brake rod from the lever arm. If necessary, disconnect the snap connector in the lead to the stop-tail light to prevent the stop light remaining on accidentally. On all 350 and 500 c.c. unit-construction models disconnect the speedometer drive cable from the gearbox.

Now unscrew the two rear-wheel spindle nuts and remove them from the spindle. Pull the rear wheel back in the frame a short distance and disconnect the chain adjusters from the rear wheel spindle. On all 1956–69 models after disconnecting the chain adjusters loosen the nut near the bottom of the near-side rear Girling suspension unit and swing the chain guard upward prior to removing the rear wheel. Now remove the rear wheel from the spring frame as shown in Fig. 39. Note that if you have a prop stand fitted, you should lower it to steady the motor-cycle during wheel removal. Some tilting of the machine is necessary. Stand on the nearside of the motor-cycle and tilt it on to the left leg of the central stand. Reach across the machine and pull the wheel clear of the fork ends.

Fitting Standard Rear Wheel (All 1956–69 Spring Frame Models). Tilt the machine to the left and position the wheel between the swinging fork, but see that the anchor plate stud is properly located in the brake torque, stay hole. Re-position the brake rod to the brake lever; fit the chain adjusters to the spindle and position the end plates; fit the chain to the sprocket and replace the connecting link; check the tension of the chain and adjust as necessary (*see* pages 78–90).

Screw the nuts on to the spindle and tighten them; fit the rear nut of the brake torque-stay and tighten both nuts: on 350 and 500 c.c. unit-construction models swing the chain guard downwards and engage it with the bolt and tighten firmly the securing nut. Finally, spin the wheel and note the operation of the brake pedal and adjust as required. Also check the wheel alignment. On 350 and 500 c.c. unit-construction models (and 650 c.c. after DU24875) fit the speedometer cable to the gearbox so that the squared end engages fully and then tighten the cable nut.

Remove Q.D. Rear Wheel (1956–62 Pre-unit-construction, 1958–62 Unit-construction Models). On 350 and 500 c.c. unit-construction models

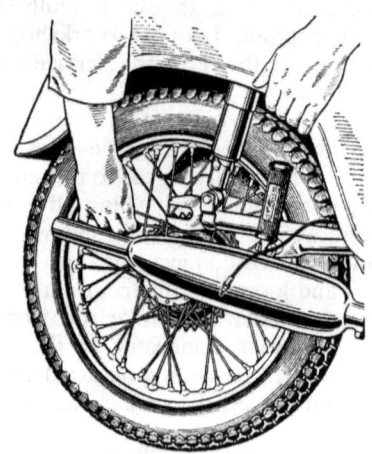

Fig. 39. Removing rear wheel from spring frame

(and 650 c.c. after DU24875) start by unscrewing the speedometer drive cable from the gearbox. Insert a suitable spanner on, or bar through, the hexagon-shaped spindle end (right-hand side) or use a spanner and unscrew until the spindle can be withdrawn. Then remove the distance piece from between the right-hand fork and the wheel.

Ease the wheel to the right-hand side until the hub splines are clear of the brake drum splines; tilt the machine to the left (pull out the prop stand if one is fitted and use as a steady) when the wheel can be removed from the right-hand side as shown in Fig. 39.

Replacing Q.D. Wheel (1956–62 Pre-unit-construction, 1958–62 Unit-Construction Models). First fit a new rubber seal over the hub splines; then, with the machine tilted over as when dismantling, enter the wheel between the forks, right the machine and locate the hub splines into the brake drum splines. Next, fit the collar with the cone-shaped end towards the hexagon to the spindle, then the chain adjuster with the stud inwards, then the distance piece between the fork and wheel and insert the spindle through the wheel and screw it into the hub sleeve.

Make sure that on 350 and 500 c.c. unit-construction models the speedometer drive is aligned with the cable. Tighten the union nut after engaging the squared end of the inner cable. Fit the chain adjuster end-plate to the right-hand adjuster stud and fork end and secure with the nut. Lastly, check the chain and brake adjustments and the wheel alignment. When correct, tighten the left-hand wheel nut and then apply a bar or spanner to the spindle hexagon and turn until the spindle is tight. Check the brake torque-stay nuts for tightness.

To Remove Q.D. Rear Wheel (All 1963–69 Unit-construction Models). On all 350 and 500 c.c., and all later 650 c.c. models first disconnect the

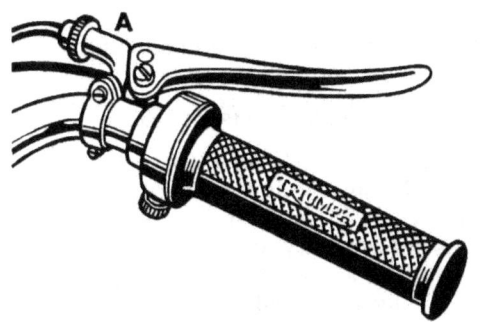

Fig. 40. The front brake adjustment

The adjustment is shown at A and applies to 1956 and later models

speedometer drive cable by unscrewing it from its drive gearbox. Unscrew the wheel spindle from the offside and drop out the distance piece between the wheel and the fork end. Pull the wheel clear of the splines on the brake drum and remove the wheel. When replacing the wheel there may be a slight variation in the fit of the splines at various points. If time permits, it is advisable to select a position which is neither tight not unduly loose and to mark this position with a small spot of paint on the brake drum and a corresponding spot on the hub. The wheel can then be easily replaced in this position at any future time. If damaged or perished renew the rubber ring which is fitted over the splines on the wheel and is compressed slightly when the spindle is tightened.

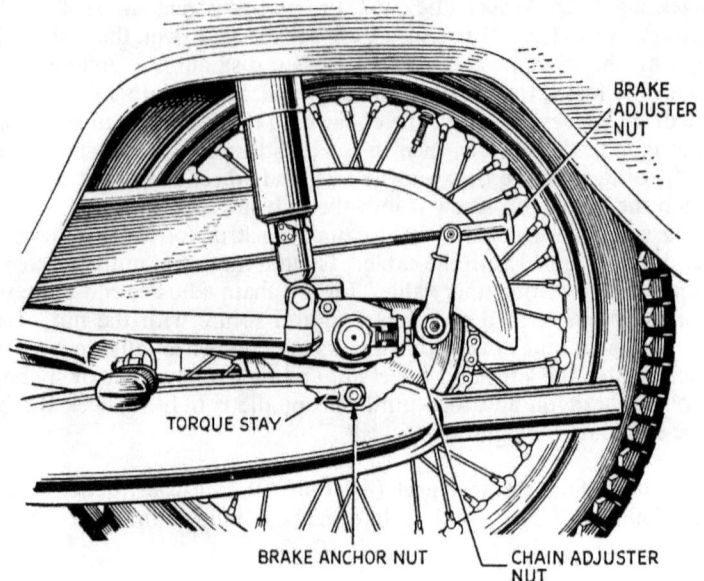

Fig. 41. The rear brake and secondary chain adjustment on 1956–69 models

The illustration shows the details on 350 and 500 c.c. unit-construction models, but the adjustments are similar on all 1956–69 machines

To Replace Q.D. Rear Wheel (All 1963–69 Unit-construction Models). The replacement of the quickly detachable rear wheel is the exact reverse of the removal procedure. If you do not alter the setting of the off-side chain adjuster it is not necessary to check wheel alignment.

If both chain adjusters are not adjusted an equal amount it is essential to check the wheel alignment and then readjust the chain adjusters as required (*see* page 80).

Adjusting Both Brakes. The wheels must be raised off the ground, before making any adjustment, by placing the machine on its stand or stands as the case may be. Adjustment is usually required every 1,000 miles.

To adjust the brake shoes closer to the brake drum, in the case of the front brake, turn the knurled thumb-nut (*A*, Fig. 40) in an *anti-clockwise* direction. The brake should be set so that when fully applied the lever is just clear of the handlebar. If this be done, the rider is able to exert the maximum amount of grip on the lever. Spin the wheel after making this adjustment to ensure that the brake shoes are not binding on the brake drum. On all 1963–69 unit-construction models an alternative cable abutment is available to compensate for cable lengths which cannot be satisfactorily allowed for by normal cable adjustments. *See* page 130.

GENERAL MAINTENANCE: THE MOTOR-CYCLE 77

The adjustment of the rear brake is made by turning the knurled thumb-nut (Fig. 41) at the rear end of the brake operating rod in a *clockwise* direction. Spin the wheel after adjusting to make certain that the brake is not binding. On later machines the rear brake pedal is adjustable for position. This adjustment should be made *before* making an adjustment with the knurled thumb nut. With the rear brake correctly adjusted there should be approximately ½ in. free movement of the pedal before the brake shoes begin to exert friction.

The Tyres. The tyres must be maintained at the correct inflation pressure if they are to provide safe and comfortable riding, a long life and

**RECOMMENDED TYRE PRESSURES
(1956-69 SOLO MODELS)**

Tyre Size (Dunlop or Avon)	Inflation pressures
Front { 3·25 × 18	20 lb per sq in.
{ 3·25 × 19	20 lb per sq in.
Rear { 3·50 × 18	20 lb per sq in.
{ 4·00 × 18	18 lb per sq in.

MINIMUM TYRE PRESSURES FOR SPECIFIC LOADS

Nominal Tyre Section (in.)	Inflation Pressures (lb per sq in.)				
	18	20	24	28	32
	Load per tyre (lb.)				
3·25	240	280	350	400	440
3·50	320	350	400	450	500
4·00	400	430	500	—	—

(*By courtesy of The Dunlop Rubber Co., Ltd.*)

immunity from trouble. The pressure should be checked every week, a reliable pressure gauge being used for the purpose. Suitable pressure gauges are the Holdtite, the Dunlop pencil-type No. 6, the Schrader 7750, and the Romac.

Where a pillion passenger is carried it is usually advisable to increase the pressure of the front tyre by 4 lb per sq in. and the pressure of the rear tyre by 6 lb per sq in. Generally speaking, it is advisable to run the rear tyre at a moderate pressure, consistent with good steering. If the tyre is too soft the machine will tend to wander, and if too hard, riding will be uncomfortable and the rear wheel will tend to bounce. The exact tyre pressures recommended depend upon the rider's weight and the type of machine, and are to some extent a matter for individual experiment.

The correct average tyre inflation pressures for 1956–69 Triumph twin-cylinder models are given above. These pressures apply to solo models and are based on the rider's weight being not more than 170 lb. Add 1 lb per sq in. for every 28 lb increase in weight above 170 lb, in the case of the front tyre. Where the rear tyre is concerned, add 1 lb per sq in. for every 14 lb increase in weight above 170 lb. Where an extra load is carried in the form of a pillion passenger or luggage, determine the actual load on each tyre (on a weighbridge at a railway station or large transport depot) and then use the minimum tyre pressures for specific loads recommended in the accompanying Dunlop table.

The tyres should be examined regularly, particularly after riding over roads which have been tarred and gritted, and any sharp pieces of stone or flint should be removed with a pen-knife. If allowed to remain, no immediate danger may be caused, but ultimately they will work right through the cover and puncture the tube.

Balanced Front Wheels. On many models from about 1963 onwards the front wheel is balanced (by weights), complete with the tube and tyre, before leaving Coventry. On these models after removing the front tyre, make sure that it is subsequently replaced in its original position, with the balancing spot *level* with the valve. If you fit a *new* tyre, remove the balance weights and re-balance the wheel (after checking that the brake shoes are not binding) by positioning the weights until the front wheel remains static when turned to any position.

CHAIN MAINTENANCE

Badly adjusted chains are a frequent cause of harsh running and excessive wear. It is therefore of great importance to see that the primary and secondary chains are correctly adjusted (check tension every 1,000 miles) and properly lubricated. Lubrication has already been dealt with in Chapter 3. On (1956–69) *"swinging arm" spring frame* models the correct primary tension is $\frac{1}{2}$ in. The correct secondary chain tension is $\frac{3}{4}$ in. with the machine off its stand or $1\frac{3}{4}$ in. *with the machine on its stand*. Chain "tension" means the total up and down chain deflection obtained with the fingers, vertically near the chain centre, with the chain in its tightest position.

Primary Chain Adjustment (1956–62 Pre-unit-construction 500 and 650 c.c. Models). The gearbox pivot secures the gearbox to the lower frame and must be slackened before adjusting the primary chain. Slacken the securing nut of the gearbox clamping bolt (*see* Fig. 42) which also positions the adjuster.* To tighten the primary chain, slacken off the front lock-nut a few turns and tighten up the rear lock-nut until the tension

*All later type pre-unit-construction models have a *duplicate* adjustment on the nearside of the gearbox. In this case the easiest method of adjusting the primary chain tension is to slacken off both adjuster lock-nuts on the left adjuster and then use the *right* adjuster for actual chain retensioning.

GENERAL MAINTENANCE: THE MOTOR-CYCLE 79

is correct; to slacken the chain, reverse the order. Lastly, re-tighten the clamp nut, lock-nuts and pivot bolt and see they are absolutely secure.

The Primary Chain (1958–60 Unit-construction 350, 500 c.c. Models). Models 3TA and 5TA have a duplex chain bedded-down during production at Coventry, and no subsequent adjustment is provided or necessary.

The Primary Chain (1960–67 Unit-construction 350, 500 and 650 c.c. Models). The primary chain is not adjustable as the engine mainshaft

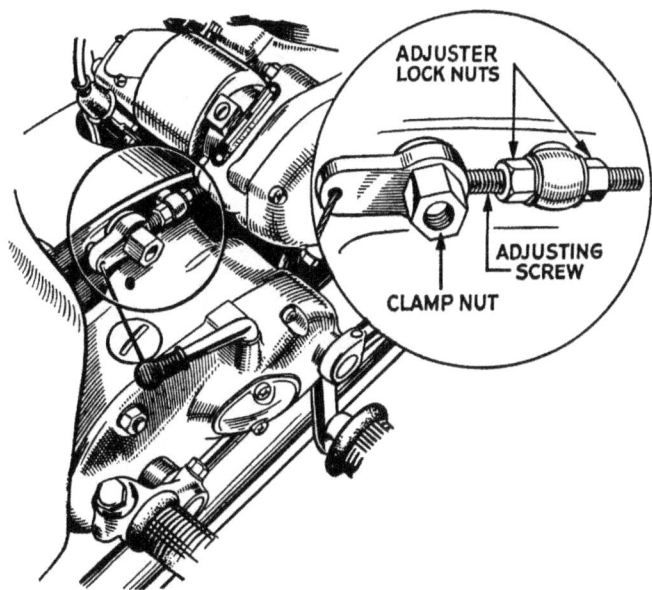

Fig. 42. Primary chain adjustment on all 1956–62 pre-unit-construction 500 and 650 c.c. models

and gearbox centres are fixed. Provision is, however, made for taking up chain wear with a rubber-faced slipper blade positioned below the chain bottom run as may be seen in Figs. 18, 19. To feel the free movement of the chain remove the top inspection plug from the oil-bath chain case and insert a finger.

While your finger is still inserted inside the case be careful not to move the chain by using the kickstarter pedal. To reduce chain slackness first place a drip-tray beneath the oil-bath chain case and remove the oil drain plug (*see* Figs. 18, 19) from the bottom of the chain case (adjacent to the central stand L.H. lug). Then with a suitable conventional-type screwdriver (*see* Fig. 43), tighten as required the slotted adjuster nut on the rear end of the tensioner. After obtaining the correct chain tension remove the screwdriver, replace the drain plug and replenish the oil-bath chain case with the recommended type and amount of oil (*see* page 35).

Secondary Chain Adjustment (Swinging-arm Models). This adjustment can be carried out with the machine off the stand.

Slacken off both wheel nuts and the brake anchor nut. The adjusters are on the wheel spindle and the swinging-fork end lugs (*see* Fig. 41). To tighten the secondary chain, turn the adjuster nuts clockwise *an equal*

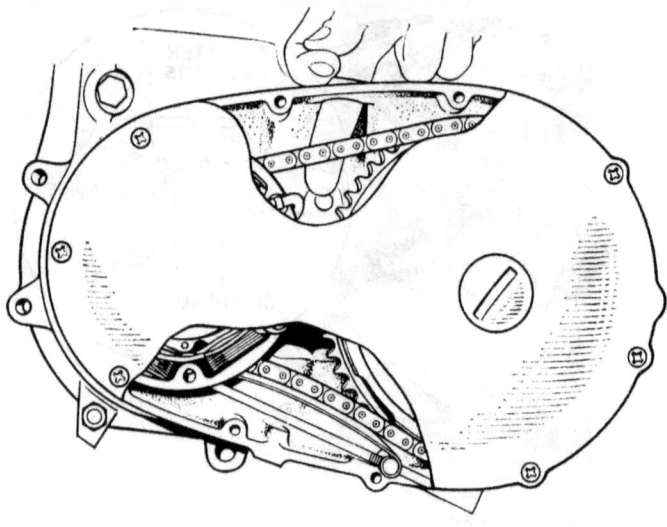

Fig. 43. Adjusting primary-chain tensioner (All 1959–69 unit-construction 350, 500 and 650 c.c. models)

(*From Triumph Workshop Manual*)

number of turns until the correct tension is secured; to slacken, reverse the order and push the wheel forward against the adjuster end plates. Finally, tighten the adjuster lock-nuts and wheel spindle nuts (also brake anchor nut).

Always depress the rear brake pedal to centralize the brake plate and maintain pressure on it while you tighten the near-side spindle nut. Afterwards check the brake adjustment and wheel alignment.

Cleaning Chains. The owner should, of course, see that both chains are properly lubricated but, in addition, the secondary chain should be removed at intervals and cleaned thoroughly and re-greased.

GENERAL MAINTENANCE: THE MOTOR-CYCLE 81

To clean and re-grease the secondary chain may take a little time, but it is well worth while doing the job properly. Take off this chain and brush off all external dirt with a wire brush. To remove dirt and old grease from the joints, soak the chain in a paraffin bath and move it about until it is thoroughly clean, then rinse it in clean paraffin and hang it up to drain and dry. After drying, re-lubricate it by immersing it in a bath of grease which has been melted over a pan of boiling water and allow it to remain for five to ten minutes, and during this period it should be moved about freely so that the grease penetrates into the bearings. When the grease has cooled to its normal state take the chain out of the bath, wipe off all surplus grease and replace the chain on the machine. Fitting the spring clip fastener on the connecting link is simple, provided the rider remembers this—the fastener is like a fish in shape—a fish swims nose first and the fastener must be fitted so that the nose (the closed end) always proceeds in the forward direction when the motor-cycle is running.

The owner is advised to clean and re-grease the secondary chain at the beginning of the winter, halfway through the winter and at the beginning of the summer.

FRAME AND SIDECAR HINTS

The "Swinging-arm" Frame. The swinging fork is pivoted to the main frame by a ground hollow spindle. Two phosphor-bronze bushes are pressed into the fork bridge lug to provide a bearing surface on which the fork swings. The spindle is a light drive fit into the frame lug and a working fit in the fork bushes. To retain the spindle in position, a rod is passed through the hollow in the spindle and at each end a retainer cap is made captive by nuts screwed on the rod ends. A spacing washer is fitted between the bridge lug and the frame lug on the right-hand side, so as to obtain the clearance which may be up to 0·015 in. when new. *Shims of* 0·003 *in. and* 0·005 *in. are available to take up excessive clearance.*

The life of the bearing bushes is approximately 20,000 miles under average running conditions. To replace the bushes is an operation of a major type and, therefore, the owner is advised to put the work in the hands of a Triumph Dealer.

Girling Hydraulic Suspension Units. These units are completely self-contained and are known under the type number SB4. They are sealed on assembly and cannot be adjusted. 1969 models have exposed springs.

If trouble occurs after a big mileage the complete units should be returned to the nearest Girling service agent whose address can be obtained from your local Triumph authorized dealer.

Should you have additional weight on the rear of your Triumph, such as a heavy pillion passenger or pannier equipment with luggage, the swinging fork member will position itself above the horizontal. The effect of this is to reduce the springing potential. To remedy this condition, you should increase the poundage in each Girling suspension damper unit by turning the spring abutment cam (*see* Fig. 44) with the *C* spanner in the tool-kit to second or third positions. The adjustment is best made with the machine on its central stand.

Wheel Alignment (Solo Models). To ensure good steering and to prevent uneven tyre wear and a skidding tendency it is essential always to keep the motor-cycle front and rear wheels in true alignment. Their alignment should remain satisfactory, provided you turn both chain-tension adjuster nuts (*see* Fig. 41) exactly the same number of turns when adjusting the tension of the secondary chain.

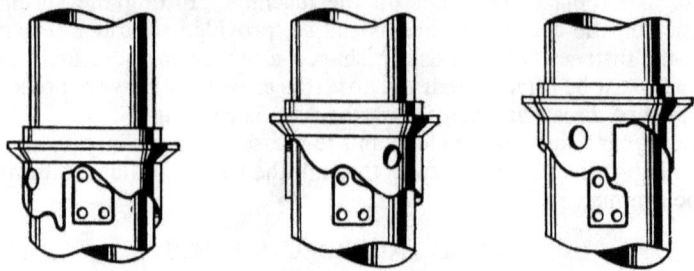

Fig. 44. Girling hydraulic suspension unit adjustment

On the left is shown the first position for a light load, in the centre the second position for a medium load, and on the right the third position for a heavy load

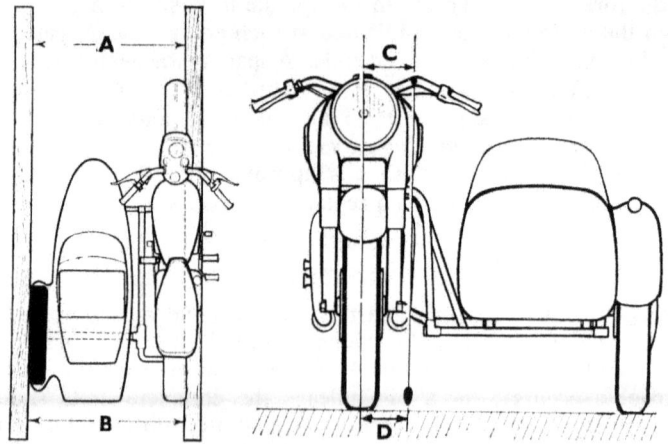

Fig. 45. Showing (left) wheel alignment check for sidecar "toe-in", and (right) dimensional check for motor-cycle "lean out"

The "toe-in" is, of course, the difference between distances A and B; the "lean-out" is the difference between distances C and D. For checking the former, two straight-edges are required, and for checking the latter a plumb line is needed

(From Triumph Workshop Manual)

GENERAL MAINTENANCE: THE MOTOR-CYCLE   83

The front and rear tyres of all 1956-67 Triumph Twins are not of the same size (*see* page 77) and therefore to check the wheel alignment it is necessary to place *two* straight-edges or battens (about five feet long, 3 inches wide, and 1 inch thick) alongside both wheels, one on each side of the motor-cycle, with the latter off its central stand. When the straight-edges contact the rear tyre at two points on both sides of the wheel, the alignment of the front and rear wheels is correct if the front tyre is found to be parallel with and midway between both the straight-edges. Adjust wheel alignment, if necessary, by means of the two tension-adjuster nuts for the secondary chain.

Wheel Alignment (Sidecar Outfits). First check the alignment of the motor-cycle front and rear wheels as just described. Then, with the sidecar outfit on a level, smooth surface, position (about 4 in. above the ground) the two previously-mentioned straight-edges alongside the rear tyre of the motor-cycle and the sidecar tyre as shown in Fig. 47. Check the difference between distances *A* and *B*. The "toe-in" of the sidecar wheel is correct if *A* is about ¾ in. less than *B*. Should "toe-in" be found incorrect, adjust the sidecar fixings as required.

The motor-cycle itself should lean out about 1 in. out of the vertical towards the off-side. This alignment can be checked as indicated in Fig. 45 by attaching a plumb line to the near-side of the handlebars and taking measurements between the plumb line and the vertical centre-line of the wheel. Distance *C* should be 1 in. more than distance *D*, and if necessary the telescopic arms of the sidecar chassis should be adjusted accordingly. As regards "toe-in," fitting a sidecar, and dealing with its maintenance, always observe precisely the sidecar-maker's instructions.

Attaching a Sidecar. Note that stronger telescopic front-fork springs are required for a sidecar outfit than for a solo model. If you attach a sidecar to a Triumph bought for solo use, take the motor-cycle to a Triumph dealer and get him to fit heavy-duty springs to the telescopic front-forks. Do not attempt to fit the springs yourself. If you own a Triumph Twin fitted with rear panels, it may also be necessary to have longer front-fork legs fitted.

THE GEARBOX AND CLUTCH

The Gearbox (1956-69 Models). The gearbox is of Triumph design and manufacture. It has four speeds and is very strongly made. Very little attention is normally required, but it is essential to keep the gearbox properly lubricated (*see* page 33). Check that the clamping-bolt nuts are tight (pre-unit-construction). Should serious gearbox trouble develop it is best to take the machine or gearbox to a Triumph dealer who undertakes repairs. Provided that the machine is handled properly, however, gearbox trouble rarely develops. Special gears are obtainable for those who wish to indulge in racing, but racing requirements are beyond the scope of this handbook which deals with touring models.

Clutch Adjustment (All 1956–62 500 and 650 c.c. Pre-unit-construction Twins). There should always be a free movement in the clutch cable of about ⅛ in. Without this free movement the clutch is liable to slip, and rapid wear of the plate inserts will inevitably occur.

Where an adjustment is necessary, screw in the adjuster inside the gearbox inspection cover (*see* Fig. 42) until there is $\frac{1}{16}$ in. free movement at the end of the operating lever. Then adjust the cable at the lug on top of the gearbox to give the required ⅛ in. free movement at the handlebars.

Clutch Adjustment (1958–67 350, 500 and 650 c.c. Unit-construction Twins). Loosen the knurled finger adjustment at the handlebar lever (*see* Fig. 2). Then loosen the lock-nut in the centre of the clutch pressure plate and screw in the adjuster until the pressure plate just starts to lift. Afterwards screw it back *one full turn*. If the gear change pedal is stiff, slacken the adjuster a little more until it becomes free. Now tighten the lock-nut. Finally turn the knurled finger-adjustment until there is approximately ⅛ in. free movement in the clutch cable. If the oil-bath chain-case cover has not been removed, you can obtain access to the slotted adjustment screw and lock-nut (*see* Figs. 18, 19) in the centre of the clutch pressure-plate by removing the slotted cap from the outside of the chain-case cover.

Clutch and Shock-absorber Unit (1956–69 Models). The clutch on all 1956–67 models is of the multi-plate type incorporating a transmission

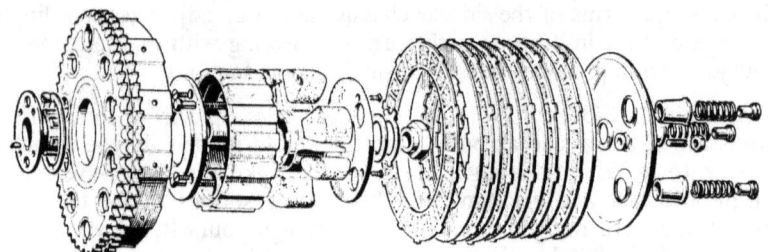

Fig. 46. Exploded view of clutch and shock-absorber unit fitted to many 350, 500 and 650 c.c. Triumph Twins

The arrangement shown is basically the same for all 1956–69 models, but there are some variations On most 1958–62 350 and 500 c.c. unit-construction models and all 1956–62 pre-unit construction 500 and 650 c.c. models 4 clutch springs are fitted. The last-mentioned also have a single type of clutch sprocket and 5 driving plates (with bonded friction material). The first-mentioned have 4 driving plates instead of the 6 illustrated

(*Triumph Engineering Co. Ltd.*)

shock-absorber. The pressure on the plates is exerted by four or three equally disposed springs, which can be adjusted by screwing in or out the four slotted nuts which secure them. It is important to see that the oil level in the chain case is maintained correctly as the clutch is designed to operate in oil; otherwise the inserts may burn and disintegrate under

GENERAL MAINTENANCE: THE MOTOR-CYCLE 85

heavy loading. Only the recommended grade of oil should be used, because if a heavier one be used, the clutch plates will not separate properly when disengaged and this causes difficult and noisy gear-selection when the foot-change pedal is used. Always operate the kickstarter a few times with the clutch withdrawn before starting the engine. This makes certain that the plates separate freely when a gear selection is made.

The shock-absorber unit is strongly constructed and is designed to give many thousands of miles of service.

To Remove and Replace Oil-bath Chain-case Cover (1956–62 Pre-unit-construction 500 and 650 c.c. Models and 1958 Unit-construction 350 and 500 c.c. Models). First remove the near-side exhaust pipe and silencer as a unit; also remove the near-side footrest. Slacken as required, or remove, the knurled adjuster nut on the rear end of the brake-operating rod, and swing the brake pedal downwards until it clears the oil-bath chain case cover. On some pre-unit-construction models it may be found necessary to remove the pedal from its shaft.

Place a suitable drip-tray beneath the oil-bath chain case, remove the drain plug and allow all oil to drain off. Then remove the screws whicn secure the chain-case cover and withdraw the cover. When doing this on models fitted with an alternator, be very careful not to damage or fray the stator windings or electrical leads (*see* Fig. 24).

Before replacing the oil-bath chain-case cover on 1956–62 pre-unit construction 500 and 650 c.c. models, check and if necessary adjust the tension of the primary chain (*see* page 78). Grease the paper gasket and then fit it to the face of the chain-case cover. Offer up the latter to the inner half of the chain case and secure by means of the screws provided. Tighten all of these screws evenly and in a diagonal order, working from the centre. Then remove the oil-filler plug and replenish the oil-bath chain case with ¼ pint of suitable oil (*see* page 35).

Replace the near-side footrest and firmly tighten its securing nut. Also replace the brake pedal, if removed, and/or connect the rod which operates the brake to the brake-cam lever by means of the knurled adjuster nut. Afterwards adjust the rear brake as described on page 76. Finally replace as a unit the near-side exhaust pipe and silencer. Make sure that this unit is firmly secured to the engine and motor-cycle.

To Remove and Replace Oil-bath Chain-Case Cover (1959–69 Unit-construction 350, 500 and 650 c.c. Models). Remove the near-side exhaust pipe and silencer as a unit. If your motor-cycle has twin exhaust pipes and silencers fitted, slacken the near-side finned-clip bolt, the silencer-clip bolt and the nut which secures the near-side exhaust-pipe bracket beneath the crankcase. Should the end of the exhaust pipe be a tight fit in the exhaust port, free it by tapping the curve of the pipe forwards, using a rubber or hide mallet.

Screw out the knurled adjuster nut on the rod which operates the rear-brake until the pedal clears the chain-case cover. Also unscrew the nut which secures the near-side footrest and remove the footrest. On 650 c.c. models having the footrest bolted to the motor-cycle frame beneath the power unit, tap the footrest sharply downwards to free it from its locking taper.

Lay a drip-tray beneath the chain-case cover and remove the oil drain plug and fibre washer (*see* Fig. 18 or 19), adjacent to the central stand lug, and allow all oil to drain from the chain case. Next unscrew and remove the slotted chain-tensioner adjuster (on 350 and 500 c.c. models), also the two domed nuts and copper washers (on 650 c.c. models) and unscrew the ten or eight (650 c.c. models) recessed screws which secure the chain-case cover. Finally withdraw the cover and remove its paper gasket.

Replace the oil-bath chain-case cover in the reverse order of removal. On 350 and 500 c.c. models after replacing the slotted chain-tensioner adjuster, adjust correctly the tension of the primary chain (*see* page 79). Prior to fitting the cover always renew the paper gasket and smear some grease (not jointing compound) on the joint *inner* surface. This will facilitate correct gasket positioning during assembly. Tighten the two domed nuts (where provided) and the ten or eight recessed screws securing the chain-case cover firmly and in a diagonal order, working from the centre. Finally replace the oil drain plug and fibre washer and pour in through the oil filler-plug hole (*see* Fig. 18 or 19) the correct amount of recommended oil (*see* page 35); this is $\frac{1}{2}$ pint for 350 and 500 c.c. models and $\frac{5}{8}$ pint for 650 c.c. models.

Removing Clutch Plates (All 1956–69 Models). As may be understood by reference to Fig. 46 and its caption, the design and general arrangement of the clutch and shock-absorber assembly is the same on all pre-unit-construction and unit-construction models, except for some variations in the number of clutch springs and driving and driven plates fitted.

Note that the three or four clutch pressure-plate springs are located in position, and the adjuster nuts prevented from turning, by location "pips" on the spring-pressure adjuster nuts and inside the cups containing the springs, on all later unit-construction models.

Assuming that the cover has already been removed from the oil-bath chain case (*see* page 85), remove the clutch plates in the following manner. First remove the external spring-pressure adjuster nuts; insert a narrow screwdriver under the head of each nut to hold the spring away from the "pip" while unscrewing the slotted nut by means of the special key or screwdriver (Part No. D364) provided in the tool-kit, or alternatively with the type of screwdriver shown in Fig. 47.

After removing the three or four adjuster nuts, withdraw the pressure springs, followed by the external pressure-plate complete with spring cups. The driving (i.e. the bonded friction) plates and the driven (plain steel) plates can then be withdrawn from the clutch housing. Removal of the clutch plates can be assisted by means of two narrow hook-tools

GENERAL MAINTENANCE: THE MOTOR-CYCLE 87

made from a piece of $\frac{1}{32}$ in. diameter wire by bending it to form a hook at one end.

No further dismantling of the clutch should be necessary if there is no evidence of the shock-absorber rubbers having worn badly and it is

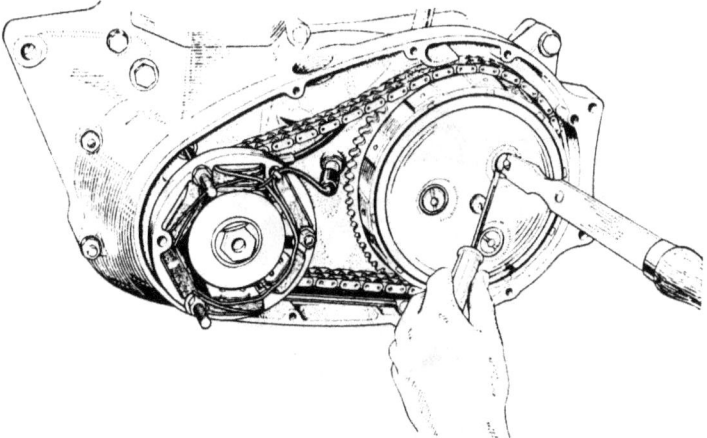

Fig. 47. Unscrewing clutch nuts which adjust the pressure-springs on a unit-construction model

(*From Triumph Workshop Manual*)

intended to replace the existing driving plates or fit service relined friction plates.

Maintenance of Shock-absorber Unit. When the cover of the oil-bath chain case, and also the clutch plates, have been removed as previously described, the shock-absorber unit is rendered accessible. This unit comprises a housing, a paddle or spider, shock-absorbing rubbers, and inner and outer cover plates. To remove the shock-absorbing rubbers it is not necessary to remove the complete shock-absorber unit. They can be removed for inspection and renewal (where necessary) in the following manner.

Unscrew the 3 or 4 screws which secure the outer cover-plate of the unit and lever out this plate with a suitable tool. Then prise out with a sharp-pointed tool the *smaller* rebound-rubbers, and afterwards withdraw the *larger* drive rubbers. The existing rubbers should be replaced if there is any definite evidence of cracking or punctures. Note that even slight punctures are likely to cause the rubbers to disintegrate ultimately, thereby ruining smooth transmission. If in any doubt, fit a complete new set of rubbers.

When fitting existing or new rubbers to the shock-absorber unit first fit all the *larger* drive-rubbers. Then fit the *smaller* rebound-rubbers using a broad-bladed screwdriver as shown in Fig. 48 to hold the spider while inserting the rubbers. On some shock-absorber units it may be necessary to lever the spider arms with a small tommy-bar to assist assembly of these rubbers. Do not use oil or grease to facilitate rubber assembly, because this is liable to reduce their effective working life.

Apply some Triumph "Loctite" to the threads of the 3 or 4 screws

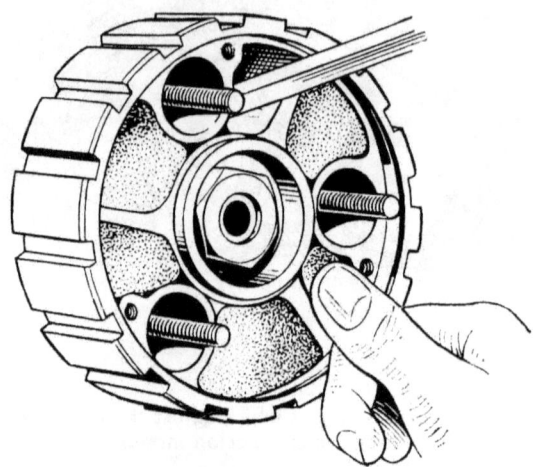

Fig. 48. Fitting the rebound rubbers to the shock-absorber unit
The large drive rubbers have already been fitted
(From Triumph Workshop Manual)

which secure the outer cover-plate prior to firmly tightening down the cover-plate, and when doing this always use a screwdriver whose blade engages the *full* depth of each screw slot.

Inspecting Clutch Plates and Springs. First thoroughly clean all components in paraffin. Then examine the driving (bonded friction) plates for wear and general condition. The segments of new plates should protrude $\frac{1}{32}$ in. on both sides of each plate and the fitting of service relined plates is not necessary unless the segments have become badly burned or until the reduction in the overall thickness of each friction plate exceeds 0·030 in. (0·75 mm).

Check that the driving-plate tags are a good fit in the clutch housing recesses and that no excessive slackness exists. The driven (plain steel) plates must be absolutely flat and have no scored surfaces. They have a bonderized finish and should never be polished.

Assembling Clutch Plates and Springs (All Models). Assemble the plates in the reverse order of removal, fitting first a *driving* (bonded friction)

GENERAL MAINTENANCE: THE MOTOR-CYCLE 89

plate, then a *driven* (plain steel) plate and so on until all the plates are assembled in the clutch housing. Make sure that the clutch push-rod is in position before fitting the outer pressure-plate complete with spring cups. Then fit the pressure springs into the cups and secure the pressure plate and clutch springs by fitting the 3 or 4 spring-pressure adjuster nuts; tighten these slotted nuts so that the threaded ends of the clutch pins are flush with their outer faces.

It is essential that the external pressure-plate *spins truly and without any "wobble"*. To check that such is the case, select neutral, sit astride your Triumph, disengage the clutch, and while turning the engine over with the kick-starter, observe the rotation of the pressure plate closely, relative to the clutch housing. If there is any sign of uneven rotation and "wobble", note the position of the "high spot" and tighten the nearest adjuster nut(s) about half a turn at a time until dead true rotation occurs. When tightening each adjuster nut, use a narrow screwdriver to hold the clutch pressure-spring away from the nut "pip" as shown in Fig. 47.

Finally attend to clutch adjustment (*see* page 84), replace the cover on the oil-bath chain case (*see* page 85) and replenish the latter with suitable oil (*see* page 35).

Spares and Repairs. The Triumph Engineering Co. Ltd., who started making Triumph motor-cycles in 1904 and in 1965 captured the world's speed record by obtaining a recorded speed on a 650 c.c. Triumph Boneville 120 of no less than 224.57 m.p.h., are justly proud of the workmanship and design of their Triumph twins. However, everything in this world depreciates and requires renewal or repair! Sooner or later your Triumph will need spares or repairs, or perhaps a major overhaul. Note the brief advice given on page 120.

6 General Maintenance: The Engine

THIS chapter deals with some important aspects of engine maintenance such as valve clearance adjustment, valve timing, ignition timing, decarbonizing, etc. For detailed information on carburettor tuning and maintenance, engine lubrication and the ignition system, *see* Chapters 2 to 4.

VALVE CLEARANCES

On *all* engines every 3,000–4,000 miles check and *if necessary* adjust the inlet and exhaust valve clearances with the engine *cold*. The maintenance of correct valve clearances is essential to obtain maximum power output, smooth and quiet running, and to prevent the valves and their seats quickly becoming pitted or damaged. Feeler gauges cannot be used for checking the clearances.

1956–62 500 and 650 c.c. Pre-unit-construction Models. The engines of these Triumph Twins have either: (*a*) camshafts of *ramp-cam* form requiring inlet and exhaust valve clearances of 0·010 in. (0·25 mm), or (*b*) *high-lift* camshafts requiring inlet and exhaust valve clearances of 0·002 in. (0·05 mm) and 0·004 in. (0·010 mm) respectively.

The actual valve-clearance adjustment, as well as the clearances, varies to some extent according to whether the engine has the type (*a*) or type (*b*) camshafts referred to above. Note that *all* engines of machines such as 6T and T110 (*after* engine D11193) with type (*a*) camshafts can be readily identified; they have a maker's symbol as shown in Fig. 49, adjacent to the engine Serial No. The valve clearances of all engines should be checked and adjusted as described below, after first removing the four inspection caps and washers from the rocker-boxes.

To position the valves, first remove the sparking plugs, then turn the engine by the kickstarter until the left exhaust valve is fully open, as this makes sure that the right exhaust valve tappet is making contact with the base of the cam, and the valve clearance at the right exhaust rocker should be set correctly. Afterwards the engine must be turned until the right exhaust valve is fully open and the valve clearance at the left exhaust rocker should be checked and adjusted. A similar sequence should be used for checking and adjusting the inlet valve clearances.

Two spanners (*see* Fig. 49) are provided in the tool-kit for adjusting

GENERAL MAINTENANCE: THE ENGINE 91

each overhead rocker adjuster-pin as required. If your engine has type (a) camshafts, observe the following instructions (1) and (2). If it has type (b) camshafts, use instructions (1) and (3) only.

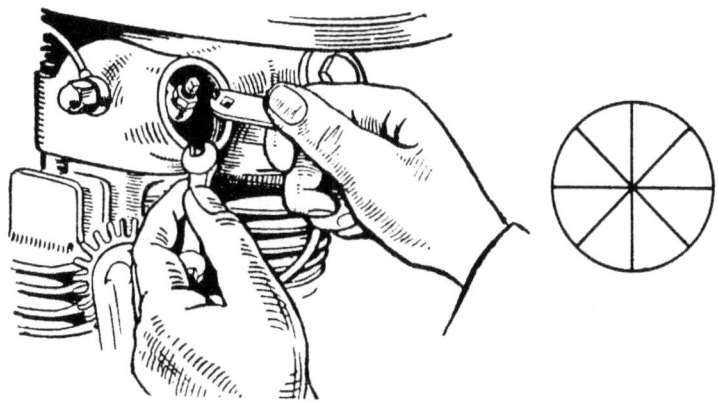

Fig. 49. Valve clearance adjustment on 1956–62 500 and 650 c.c. pre-unit-construction models

On the right is the maker's symbol (adjacent to the engine serial No.), on the L.H. side of the crankcase just below the cylinder-block flange, indicating an engine fitted with ramp-cam form camshafts (referred to as type (a) in the text). This symbol is also found on all 1958–66 3TA, 5TA engines except the 1966 5TA engine and 1956–62 6T and T110 models from engine No. D11193

1 Slacken the rocker adjuster-pin lock-nut and screw down the adjuster until it just contacts the valve tip.
When the adjuster contacts the valve tip, hold the adjuster firmly with the spanner and tighten up the lock-nut with the other spanner, then grip the rocker adjuster between the thumb and forefinger and move the rocker sideways to test for freedom of movement and test the up-and-down movement where the clearance between the adjuster and valve tip should be just perceptible.
2 So that 0·010 in. (0·25 mm) clearance may be obtained, first take note of the position of the squared end of the adjuster and with both spanners in position, slacken the lock-nut slightly, but do not move the adjuster. Then slacken off the adjuster one flat (*one quarter of a turn*) and, maintaining it in the new position, re-tighten the lock-nut. Use the same procedure for each valve clearance adjustment.
3 Estimate the correct valve clearance by first adjusting the overhead rocker adjuster-pin as described in preceeding instructions (1). Then to obtain the correct exhaust valve clearance (0·004 in.), slacken the adjuster-pin *half a flat* (one-eighth of a turn). This may possibly cause a very slightly excessive exhaust-valve clearance, but this is far better than a slightly insufficient clearance. To adjust the inlet valve clearance, slightly slacken off the adjuster-pin so that when holding

the overhead rocker between the thumb and forefinger, and moving it up and down, a distinct "click" is audible when the adjuster-pin hits the tip of the valve.

1958–69 350 and 500 c.c. Unit-construction Models. First remove both sparking plugs (to free engine compression) and also remove the four slotted inspection caps and their washers from the rocker-boxes to give

Fig. 50. Valve clearance adjustment on 1958–69 350 and 500 c.c. unit-construction models

access to the overhead rocker adjuster-pins and lock-nuts. Then slacken these lock-nuts, engage top gear and proceed to check and if necessary adjust the inlet and exhaust valve clearances in this order. Two spanners (*see* Fig. 50) are provided for dealing with the square-headed adjuster-pins and their lock-nuts.

Inlet-valve Clearances. Turn the rear wheel *forwards* until the R.H. inlet valve is fully open. In this position the tappet actuating the L.H. inlet valve rests on the base circle diameter of the cam form. Then check and if necessary adjust the clearance for the *left* inlet valve, turning the rocker adjuster-pin as necessary to obtain the correct clearance in accordance with the following—

On model 3TA the required inlet-valve clearance is 0·010 in. (0·25 mm). To get this clearance, set the rocker adjuster-pin so that there is no vertical clearance between the L.H. rocker pin and the tip of the inlet valve. Then screw back the adjuster-pin *one flat* (one-quarter of a turn) and hold it in this position with the key-spanner while tightening the lock-nut.

On models 5TA, T90, T100A and T100S/S the correct inlet-valve

GENERAL MAINTENANCE: THE ENGINE

clearance is 0·002 in. (0·05 mm). This is equivalent to the slightest perceptible movement of the overhead rocker accompanied by a faint "click" on taking up the clearance between the adjuster-pin and valve tip by moving the rocker with the fingers.

As soon as you have obtained the correct clearance for the left inlet valve, again turn the rear wheel *forwards* until the L.H. inlet valve opens fully. Then check and if necessary adjust the clearance for the *right* inlet valve, using the same procedure as for the other valve.

Exhaust-valve Clearances. Having dealt with inlet-valve clearances, deal with those for the exhaust valves in a similar manner, starting with the *left* exhaust valve. Note the following—

On model 3TA the clearance required for both valves is 0·010 in. (0·25 mm), the same as for the model 3TA inlet valves. The method of adjustment is the same.

On models 5TA, T90, T110A and T100S/S the two exhaust valves both require a clearance of 0·004 in. (0·010 mm). First adjust the R.H. overhead rocker adjuster-pin to give a *nil* clearance and then screw it back *half a flat* (one-eighth of a turn). While tightening the lock-nut hold the adjuster-pin in this position.

1963–69 650 c.c. Unit-construction Twins. On 650 c.c. unit-construction twins there are four adjusters on the overhead rockers which are accessible after removing the four inspection caps from the rocker boxes. Always check valve clearances with engine *cold*. For Models 6T, TR6, T110 and T120 the correct inlet and exhaust valve clearances are 0·002 in. and 0·004 in. respectively. To ensure the correct piston position in order to check valve clearance it is best to place the Triumph on its centre stand, engage fourth gear and remove the sparking plugs. *See* page 90 re 6T and T110.

The correct procedure for checking inlet valve clearance is as follows. Rotate the rear wheel until one of the inlet overhead rockers moves downwards, thus opening the valve. When this valve is fully open the operating mechanism of the other inlet valve will be seated on the base of the cam. The valve clearance can now be checked with a "cranked" feeler gauge and adjusted if necessary, using the two tools shown in Fig. 51 and supplied in the tool kit. With a valve clearance of 0·002 in. only the slightest perceptible movement of the overhead rocker can be made with the fingers and only a faint click can be heard when the clearance is taken up. After adjusting the valve clearance for one inlet valve rotate the rear wheel until the valve just dealt with is fully open and proceed to check the valve clearance and if necessary make an adjustment for the other inlet valve. See that both rocker adjuster-pin lock-nuts are firmly re-tightened, again check the valve clearances and afterwards replace the two inspection caps. See that the fibre washers are in good condition and the inspection caps tight.

After checking and if necessary adjusting the inlet valve clearances deal with the clearances for both exhaust valves. The correct procedure is the same as for checking the inlet valve clearances, i.e. open one valve fully while you check the clearance for the other valve. To obtain a valve clearance of 0·004 in. loosen each lock-nut and adjust the rocker adjuster-pin to give a clearance of *nil*. Then turn back the adjuster one eighth of a turn (half a flat) on the squared adjuster. Hold the adjuster in this position while tightening the lock-nut. Deal with the exhaust valve similarly.

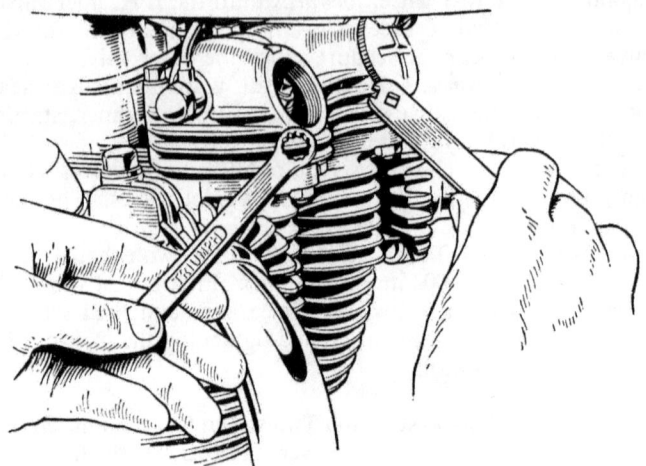

Fig. 51. Valve clearance adjustment on 1963–69 unit-construction 650 c.c. engines

Applies to Models 6T, TR6 and T120

After making each valve clearance adjustment it is important to check that the rocker adjuster-pin lock-nut is firmly tightened. Finally replace the rocker inspection caps and tighten them firmly. If the fibre washers have deteriorated, renew them.

VALVE TIMING

Punch marks are impressed adjacent to certain teeth on the crankshaft pinion intermediate gear, and camwheels to enable the owner to restore the valve timing correctly in the event of the camwheels being removed. Removal is, however, rarely necessary. Never attempt to alter the maker's valve timing. It is the best obtainable!

Checking for Correct Valve Timing. Provided that the maker's marks on and between teeth of the timing gears are correctly aligned (*see* Figs. 52, 53), it should not normally be necessary to check the valve timing of a Triumph used for touring purposes. However, if a machine is used for high speed racing or sprinting events on special fuels, or the teeth of the timing gears have become badly worn after a *very* big mileage, or the timing-gear marks have for some reason been altered, checking for correct valve timing becomes necessary, and possibly re-timing, afterwards.

GENERAL MAINTENANCE: THE ENGINE 95

To check the valve timing (not dealt with in detail in this maintenance handbook because of the rare occasions when it becomes necessary), it is essential to fit a degree timing disc to the crankshaft to determine accurately the amount of opening and closing of the inlet and exhaust valves. The correct procedure to use is fully described in the appropriate Triumph Instruction Manual or Workshop Manual. Where a valve-timing diagram is included, *never* use its valve opening and closing in degree figures of crankshaft rotation (*before and after T.D.C. and B.D.C.*), but refer to the degree figures recommended on the appropriate *Technical Data* page for *checking* the timing with a 0·020 in. (0·5 mm) valve clearance. This will prevent the valve timing being incorrectly checked and the engine afterwards behaving erratically.

Where a Triumph Twin is to be used for sporting events or racing, maximum engine performance is required and you should adjust the valve timing and check it as described in the special "Tuning" Bulletin obtainable from the Triumph Engineering Co. Ltd.

The Marking of the Timing Gears. The camwheels, intermediate gear, and the engine pinion, as previously mentioned, are all conveniently

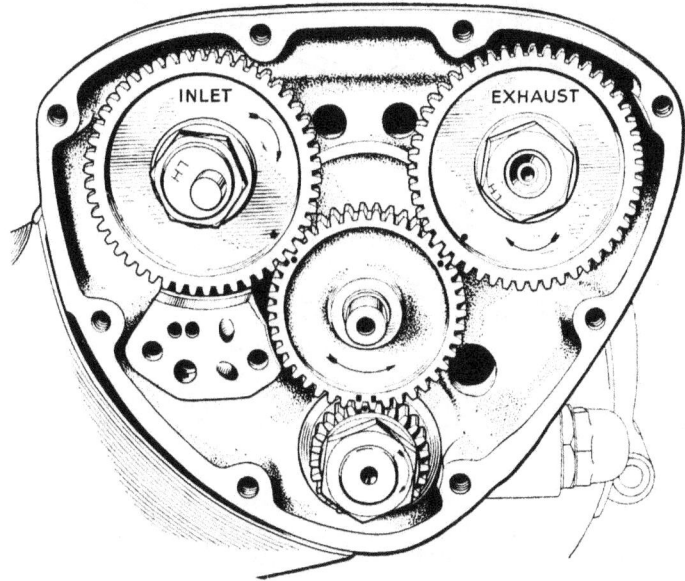

Fig. 52. Showing correct alignment of timing gear marks for 1956–62 500 c.c. pre-unit-construction models 5T, 5TA, and T100, and all 1958–69 350 and 500 c.c. unit-construction models

Note that on most earlier engines the inlet and exhaust camwheels have their single dot marks punched on their teeth peripheries instead of on the camwheel bosses as shown above
(From Triumph Workshop Manual)

marked. Each camwheel has one *dot* mark. The engine pinion also has one dot mark. The intermediate gear has dot and dash marks and these require for all normal touring purposes alignment with the dot marks on the camwheels and crankshaft pinion as indicated in Figs. 52, 53. Note

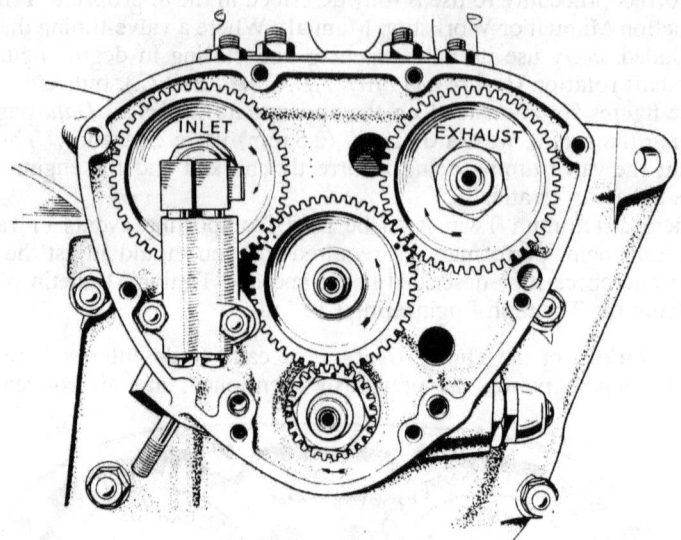

Fig. 53. Showing correct alignment of timing gear marks for 1956–69 650 c.c. pre-unit-construction and unit-construction models

Note the following differences: on all 1956–62 pre-unit-construction models the single dot on the crankshaft pinion requires alignment with twin dots on the intermediate gear instead of with the twin dash marks shown above. In the case of the inlet camwheel the single dot mark requires alignment with the short dash mark on the intermediate gear (as shown) for the 1963–6 unit-construction Model 6T; but for all other 1956–69 pre-unit-construction and unit-construction models (excluding Model 6T) the camwheel dot mark aligns with the long dash mark adjacent to the dot mark or short dash mark on the intermediate gear

(From Triumph Workshop Manual)

that the intermediate gear has a prime number of teeth and consequently the timing marks align only every 94th revolution during crankshaft rotation.

IGNITION TIMING

Checking the ignition timing, if it becomes suspect, is a simple matter, but retiming the ignition after removing the contact-breaker, disturbing its drive or undertaking considerable dismantling is not always so easy, especially on certain models. However, retiming on all recent 350, 500 and 650 c.c. Triumphs is greatly facilitated as a locating peg in the exhaust camshaft engages a slot in the contact-breaker base.

Correct retiming procedure varies considerably on 1956–69 pre-unit-construction and unit-construction models and if retiming becomes a

GENERAL MAINTENANCE: THE ENGINE 97

"must" and you experience any difficulty, you should consult the appropriate Triumph Instruction Manual, Owner's Handbook or Workshop Manual. It is impossible for the author to delve here into full details of retiming the ignition on 1956-69 power units, but some advice on checking the timing may prove helpful. Never attempt to alter the maker's recommended timing given in the two accompanying tables. Retiming fortunately is seldom necessary.

Checking Timing (1956-67 Engines). This can be done for *either* cylinder. First remove the overhead-rocker inspection caps and both sparking plugs. Then engage top gear and slowly rotate the rear wheel in its normal direction for travel. Watch the valve operation in the L.H. or R.H.

MAGNETO-IGNITION TIMINGS FOR 1956-59 ENGINES
(Showing correct distance of L.H. piston before T.D.C. when the contacts of the contact-breaker for the L.H. cylinder commence to open)

Model	TR5	TR6	T100	T110	T120
Ignition on full advance	$\frac{15}{32}$ in. before T.D.C.	$\frac{23}{64}$ in. before T.D.C.	$\frac{3}{8}$ in. before T.D.C.	$\frac{27}{64}$ in. before T.D.C.	$\frac{7}{16}$ in. before T.D.C.

cylinder. When the *inlet* valve closes, gently rotate the rear wheel until the piston in the cylinder to be dealt with is at the top of its stroke (top-dead-centre or T.D.C.). The T.D.C. position can be accurately determined by inserting a timing stick or rod through the sparking-plug hole and observing when no movement occurs on slightly rocking the rear wheel to and fro. When you find the true T.D.C. position of the piston, mark the lowest position of the timing stick or rod visible at its entry into the cylinder head, and scratch or write another mark (*see* the accompanying tables for the appropriate fraction of an inch) *above* the first mark. Insert the timing stick or rod into the sparking plug hole, preferably using a suitable guide, or better still a proprietary T.D.C. indicator, and then rotate the rear wheel backwards until the piston has descended about one inch; then reverse the engine rotation and slowly bring the piston up to the required distance, as indicated by the upper mark exactly taking up the position of the first mark. This will eliminate any error due to backlash in the timing gears.

Remove the distributor or contact-breaker cover and fully advance the manual ignition lever, if provided, on the handlebars. Where an automatic timing device is fitted (to contact breaker), wedge the unit lightly against the spring into the fully advanced position. Then check that the contacts of the contact-breaker (*see* Figs. 23, 26–8) for the cylinder being dealt with are just breaking. To verify the exact point of contact opening, slip an appropriate feeler gauge (about 0·0015 in.), or a cellophane slip, between the contacts and observe if either can readily be withdrawn (without moving the contacts) with the L.H. or R.H. piston the correct distance before T.D.C. Before checking the ignition timing it is *always*

COIL-IGNITION TIMINGS FOR 1956-67 ENGINES

(Showing correct distance of R.H. piston before T.D.C. when the contacts of the contact-breaker for the R.H. cylinder begin to open). See also page 127.

Model	Piston position before T.D.C. with ignition fully advanced
5T and 6T	$\frac{3}{32}$ in. B.T.D.C., except on 650 c.c. 6T engines numbered DU 101–5824 when timing should be $\frac{1}{64}$ in. B.T.D.C.
3TA and 5TA	At T.D.C. except on engines *after* serial No. H 32465 when the timing should be 0·010 in. B.T.D.C.
T90	$\frac{1}{64}$ in. B.T.D.C. except *after* engine No. H 32465 when the timing should be 0·060 in. B.T.D.C.
T100A	$\frac{1}{64}$ in. B.T.D.C., or $\frac{1}{16}$ in. B.T.D.C. where energy-transfer ignition is specified
T100S/S	$\frac{1}{64}$ in. B.T.D.C. or $\frac{1}{16}$ in. B.T.D.C. with an energy-transfer ignition system. After engine No. H 32465 the timing should be 0·060 in. B.T.D.C.
TR6 and T120	$\frac{3}{32}$ in. B.T.D.C. up to engine No. DU 5824, and $\frac{1}{16}$ in. B.T.D.C. on all later type touring engines

abvisable to check that the contact-breaker gap is correct with the contacts *fully* open (*see* pages 46, 50, 53, 54 or 126).

DECARBONIZING AND GRINDING-IN VALVES

The removal of carbon deposits is necessary only when the engine shows definite signs of requiring decarbonizing. The necessity for decarbonizing is indicated by a gradual falling off in power (especially on hills), a tendency for "pinking" (injurious to the engine), some loss of compression, rather noisy running, a somewhat "woolly" exhaust, more difficult starting, and a tendency for the sparking plugs to become dirty quickly. Under normal running conditions the engine will probably run at least 10,000 miles between the decarbonizing periods. Valve grinding can conveniently be done when decarbonizing, and the valves and their seats should always then be inspected.

Note that *it is entirely unnecessary to remove the cylinder block each time the engine is decarbonized.* The makers strongly advise that the cylinder block is not disturbed unless it is proposed to fit new piston rings or do some other work on the engine which requires that the cylinder block be removed. Unless the piston rings are in bad condition, and engine compression has much deteriorated, the renewal of the piston rings is quite unnecessary and the engine will run more smoothly and give better service if the rings are not touched.

Prior to stripping down the engine for a top overhaul, clean the parts about to be removed thoroughly, using paraffin or a proprietary degreasing agent. Also obtain two boxes, one for the cylinder head and associated parts, and the other for nuts, washers, etc. This will avoid waste of time searching for lost parts during the assembly of the engine. If care is taken,

GENERAL MAINTENANCE: THE ENGINE 99

decarbonizing is a straightforward and fairly simple job. Gasket sets are available for all Triumph Twins, and before commencing decarbonizing get the correct set for your own particular model.

Removing Cylinder Head (All 1956–62 500 and 650 c.c. Pre-unit-construction Models). Dismantle as follows—

Petrol Tank: turn off the petrol tap or taps and disconnect the petrol pipes. Loosen the nut securing the front of the strap which holds the tank in place and then remove the rear cross-bolt. The tank and its four rubber buffers can now be withdrawn.

Exhaust System: slacken the exhaust-pipe finned clip bolts, remove the pipe to bracket bolts, the silencer steady to frame nuts and the silencer hanger bolts. Remove each pipe and silencer as an assembly. (On models TR5 and TR6 the branch-pipe clip bolt should also be slackened and the near-side pipe and silencer taken off first.)

Torque Stays: detach the torque stays after removing the two securing nuts and frame bolts (Model T120). They comprise a flat plate supporting the carburettor float chamber. Remove the plate, float chamber, and petrol pipes as a unit.

Electrical Equipment: disconnect the h.t. leads and remove the sparking plugs.

Carburettor—Amal: remove the air filter connexion and remove the two flange nuts. Withdraw the carburettor from the fixing studs and tie it to the frame. If it is desired to clean the unit, unscrew the knurled ring securing the throttle and air slides and take away the mixing chamber assembly. Carefully tie the slide assembly to the frame, out of harm's way.

Carburettor—S.U.: remove the air filter connexion and vent pipe from the carburettor. Unscrew the flange nuts and disconnect the throttle cable at the carburettor body when the carburettor can be removed.

Rocker Feed Pipe: unscrew the acorn nuts securing the rocker oil-feed pipe banjos to the rocker spindles and then ease the pipe off the spindles.

Rocker Drain Pipe (Model 6T): slacken the adaptor bolts at the push-rod covers and remove the adaptor bolts at the cylinder head.

Rocker-boxes: after removing the four inspection caps from the two rocker-boxes, remove the six nuts (four on Model 6T) securing the rocker-boxes to the cylinder head. Their removal is *essential* to prevent damaging the cylinder-head lugs. Next remove the four small bolts and unscrew the four central cylinder-head bolts. To enable these bolts to be lifted past the top tube of the frame, raise each rocker-box as far as possible and tilt it to either side as required. Withdraw each rocker-box and its gasket from the cylinder head.

Cylinder Head: unscrew the remaining four holding-down bolts, when the head can be lifted off the block, complete with push-rod cover tubes.

Push-rods and Covers: remove.

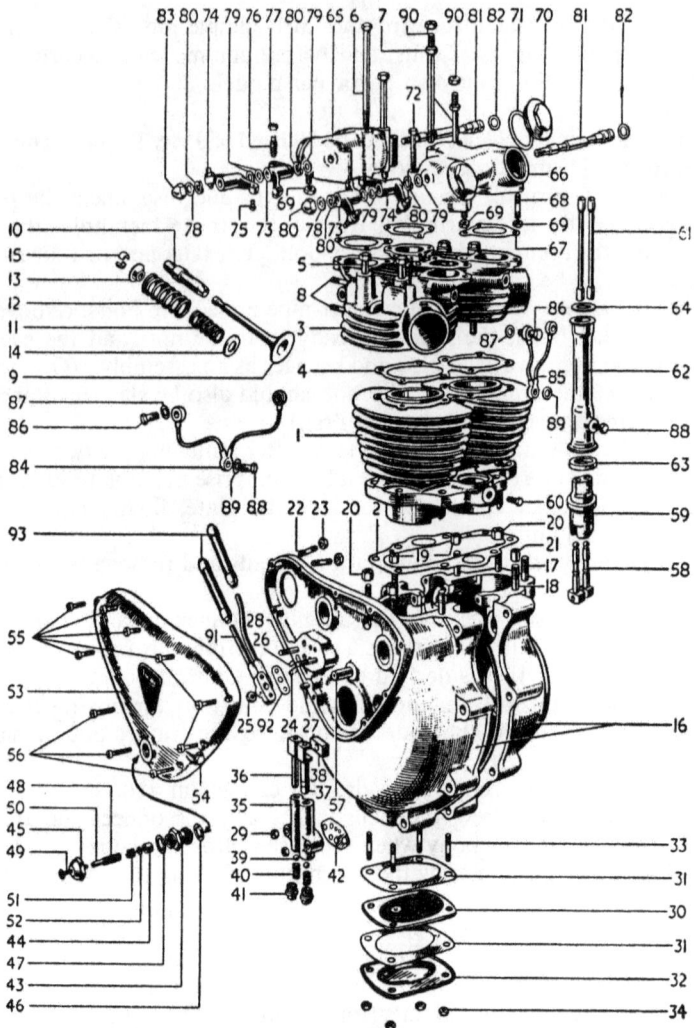

Fig. 54. Exploded view of pre-unit-construction 500 or 650 c.c. engine

Except for slight differences the 1962 engine illustrated is the same on 1956–62 models 5T, 6T, T100, T110, T120, TR5, TR6 and TR6S/S. A key to the numbered parts is opposite

(By courtesy of the Triumph Engineering Co., Ltd.)

To Replace Cylinder Head (All 1956–62 500 and 650 c.c. Pre-unit-construction Models). The following is a brief summary of the correct assembly procedure—

GENERAL MAINTENANCE: THE ENGINE

Push-rod Cover Tubes: position these after renewing their rubber washers. Note that the locating discs must have their push-rod holes *across* the machine.

Cylinder Head: renew the gasket unless the old one is in perfect condition, and then position the cylinder head on the cylinder block. Insert the four outer bolts which secure the head and tighten these finger-tight only. If you fit a used gasket, first anneal it.

Inlet Rocker-box: renew the gasket if necessary and stick it to the rocker-box face after smearing the latter with some grease. Lay the two inlet push-rods on the corresponding tappets and slowly turn the engine forwards until both tappets have descended as far as possible. Hold the inlet rocker-box slightly above the cylinder head and insert the torque-stay bolts singly while tilting the rocker-box. Carefully engage the arms

(*Key to Fig. 54*)

1. Cylinder block
2. Cylinder base washer
3. Cylinder head
4. Cylinder head gasket
5. Short bolt
6. Medium length bolt
7. Long bolt
8. Inlet manifold studs
9. Valve
10. Valve guide
11. Valve inner spring
12. Valve outer spring
13. Valve collar
14. Valve spring cup
15. Valve spring cotter
16. Crankcase halves
17. Cylinder-base stud
18. Cylinder-base stud (dowel)
19. Nut for stud
20. Nut for stud
21. Cylinder-base stud dowel
22. Magneto to crankcase stud
23. Nut for stud
24. Oil junction block stud
25. Nut for stud
26. Oil junction block dowel
27. Timing cover dowel
28. Oil pump studs
29. Nut for stud
30. Oil filter
31. Filter cover joint washer
32. Filter cover
33. Filter cover stud
34. Studs for nuts
35. Oil pump body
36. Oil pump feeder plunger
37. Oil pump scavenge plunger
38. Oil pump slider block
39. Oil pump non-return valve balls
40. Oil pump valve spring
41. Oil pump plug
42. Oil pump washer
43. Oil pressure release valve body
44. Release valve piston
45. Release valve cap
46. Washer for 43
47. Cap washer
48. Main spring
49. Oil-pressure indicator shaft
50. Rubber tube
51. Auxiliary spring
52. Shaft nut
53. Timing cover
54. Timing cover plug
55. Short screw
56. Long screw
57. Intermediate wheel spindle
58. Tappets
59. Guide block
60. Lock screw
61. Push-rods
62. Cover tube
63. Lower washer
64. Upper washer
65. Inlet rocker box
66. Exhaust rocker-box
67. Rocker-box gasket
68. Rocker-box stud
69. Nut for stud
70. Inspection cap
71. Cap washer
72. Rocker-box bolts
73. R.H. valve rocker
74. L.H. valve rocker
75. Rocker ball pin
76. Valve clearance adjuster-pii.
77. Lock-nut
78. Thrust washer
79. Thrust washer
80. Spring washer
81. Rocker spindle
82. Spindle seal
83. Dome nut
84. Oil drain pipe for inlet rockers (1956–60)
85. Oil drain pipe for exhaust rockers (1956–60)
86. Adaptor (head to pipe)
87. Washer
88. Adaptor (pipe 84 to cover-tube 62)
89. Washer
90. Torque stay nut
91. Pipes and block (oil tank to engine)
92. Oil pipe block washer
93. Oil pipe connexion (rubber)

of the overhead inlet-rockers with the push-rod ends and lower the rocker-box on to the face of the cylinder head. Screw down its securing bolts. Insert the two short bolts and replace the three nuts (two on Model 6T).

Rocker Drain Pipe (Model 6T): fit the adaptors with annealed copper washers, and tighten the adaptor bolts carefully without using excessive force.

Exhaust Rocker-box: Assemble as previously described for the inlet rocker-box.

Cylinder Head Securing Bolts: tighten these bolts firmly in a diagonal order, commencing with the four *central* bolts. The correct torque loading is 18 lb/ft. Also tighten firmly the two short rocker-box bolts and the three nuts (two on Model 6T). Finally check that the four push-rods are correctly fitted and engaged by observing the action of each valve as the engine is turned by means of the kick-starter. Replace both sparking plugs and connect the two h.t. leads.

Valve Clearances: adjust these as described on page 90 and then fit and tighten the four rocker-box inspection caps.

Torque Stays: replace these and tighten their fixings.

Carburettor—Amal: if this has been dismantled and re-assembled, verify that the throttle and air slides move freely, and replace the carburettor (*see* page 19). On all engines fit a rubber "O" ring seal in the groove provided on the face of the carburettor flange. Also on all engines having a light-alloy head fit a new gasket (a paper washer) and insulating block (*see* Fig. 7). Offer up the carburettor to the induction manifold and tighten its two flange nuts firmly but alternately. Afterwards again check the slides for free movement. If sticking occurs, suspect some distortion of the carburettor flange or excessive tightening of its securing nuts. Finally re-connect the air filter (where fitted).

Carburettor—S.U.: on a 1956–8 Model 6T fit the flange washer, assemble the S.U. carburettor to the inlet manifold, and connect up the air filter and vent pipe. Replace and tighten firmly but evenly the two carburettor flange nuts; finally assemble the throttle cable to the body of the carburettor and check for proper functioning.

Rocker Feed and Drain Pipes: replace the overhead-rocker feed pipe. Fit new copper washers and when tightening the acorn nuts securing the pipe banjos to the rocker spindles, apply a spanner to the flats on the banjos to prevent the latter turning. On Model 6T assemble the rocker drain pipe and firmly tighten the adaptor bolts.

Petrol Tank: after correctly positioning the three small and one large rubber buffers, fit the tank to the frame. When doing this, see that it does not trap any control cables or the overhead-rocker feed pipe. Replace the rear cross-bolt and tighten the front securing nut just enough to hold the tank on its rubber buffers. Tighten the tank-securing strap, but avoid excessive tightening; very slight movement of the tank is permissible. Finally assemble and connect the petrol pipes, being careful not to over-stress the unions.

GENERAL MAINTENANCE: THE ENGINE 103

Exhaust System: replace each exhaust pipe and silencer as a unit and make sure that all bracket bolts, silencer-steady nuts and hanger bolts are very firmly tightened.

After Assembly: start up your engine and allow it to warm up at a moderate speed. If necessary, make a carburettor slow-running adjustment (*see* pages 13, 23). After allowing the engine to cool right down, check all external bolts and nuts for tightness.

Removing Cylinder Head (All 1958–65 350 and 500 c.c. Unit-construction models to Engine No. H 40527). The following dismantling procedure is necessary—

Petrol Tank: turn off the petrol tap and disconnect the pipe at its

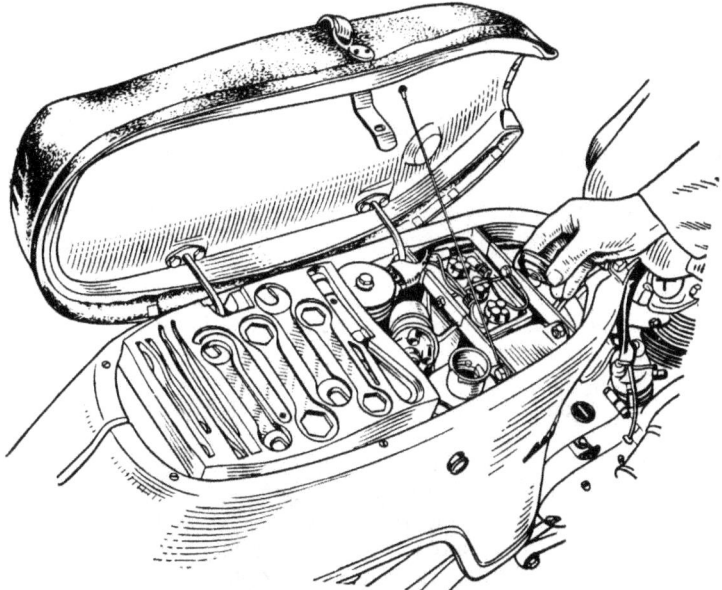

Fig. 55. Hinged twinseat raised (all 350, 500 and 650 c.c. unit-construction-models

This gives access to the oil tank filler-cap, the battery and tool tray (tool bag on recent models) it is also necessary preliminary to petrol tank removal when decarbonizing

union. Raise the twinseat (*see* Fig. 55) to obtain access to the rear bolt, and remove the two bolts and nuts which secure the petrol tank to the frame. Now remove the petrol tank.

Exhaust System: slacken the finned clips. Also remove the small bolts from the supporting stays and silencer hanger bolts. Remove each pipe and silencer as an assembly.

Amal Carburettor: remove the air filter connexion and unscrew the two flange nuts. Withdraw the carburettor from the fixing studs and tie it to the frame. Should you desire to clean the instrument (*see* page 18), unscrew the knurled ring securing the throttle and air slides and take away the mixing chamber assembly. Carefully tie the slide assembly to the frame so that it is out of the way.

Torque Stays: remove the engine torque stays.

Rocker Oil Feed Pipes: remove the acorn nuts and long bolts which secure the oil feed pipes to the rocker-box.

Rocker Boxes: unscrew the four nuts which secure the rocker-boxes to the cylinder head *before* removing the *four* Phillips screws and the four long bolts which also secure the cylinder head to the cylinder block. Lift out the push-rods.

The Cylinder Head: unscrew the four short cylinder head-to-block bolts, lift the cylinder head a little way, and then lift the push-rod cover tubes and swing their upper ends outwards in order to lift off the cylinder head.

To Replace Cylinder Head (All 1958–65 350 and 500 c.c. Unit-construction Models to Engine No. H 40527). Assemble the unit as follows—

Cylinder Head: fit new rubber washers inside the bottom of the push-rod cover tubes. Place them over the tappet blocks but not fully home. Anneal the cylinder-head gasket by heating to cherry red and plunging it into cold water. Fit new silicone rubber washers in the groove in the cylinder head and place the head in position, swinging the tops of the push-rod cover tubes outwards to place the head in position. Make sure that the push-rod cover tubes are pressed well down and that their upper ends are seating properly in the grooves in the cylinder head. Fit the four short outer cylinder-head bolts and washers and screw them down finger-tight.

Inlet Rocker Box: place the push-rods in position with the cupped ends uppermost and make sure that they are located in the tappets. Grease the joint washer and place it on the rocker box, over the studs. Place the rocker box in position and make sure that the rockers engage with the push-rods. Secure the rocker box with the Phillips screws and two nuts.

Exhaust Rocker-box: use a similar assembly procedure as for the inlet rocker-box. Now insert the four long cylinder-head bolts and washeer (torque stay bolts in the front) and tighten down the eight cylinder-head bolts, starting from the inner bolts and working diagonally across the cylinder head.

Rocker Oil Feed Pipes: fit the long bolts and acorn nuts, complete with annealed copper washers at the bolt heads, under the banjo union and under the nut.

Torque Stays: replace and secure the torque stays.

Amal Carburettor: check that the throttle slide works freely in the carburettor. Fit a new "O" ring to the carburettor, and a paper washer and the insulating block to the manifold. Tighten the nuts evenly.

GENERAL MAINTENANCE: THE ENGINE   105

Valve Clearances: adjust the valve clearances as described on page 92, and replace the inspection caps with new joint washers.

Plug Leads: replace the sparking plug leads. The lead from the front of the distributor connects to the right sparking plug, and the lead from the rear of the distributor to the left sparking plug.

Exhaust System: replace the exhaust pipes and silencers.

Petrol Tank: replace the petrol tank and re-connect the petrol pipe to the tap and carburettor float chamber.

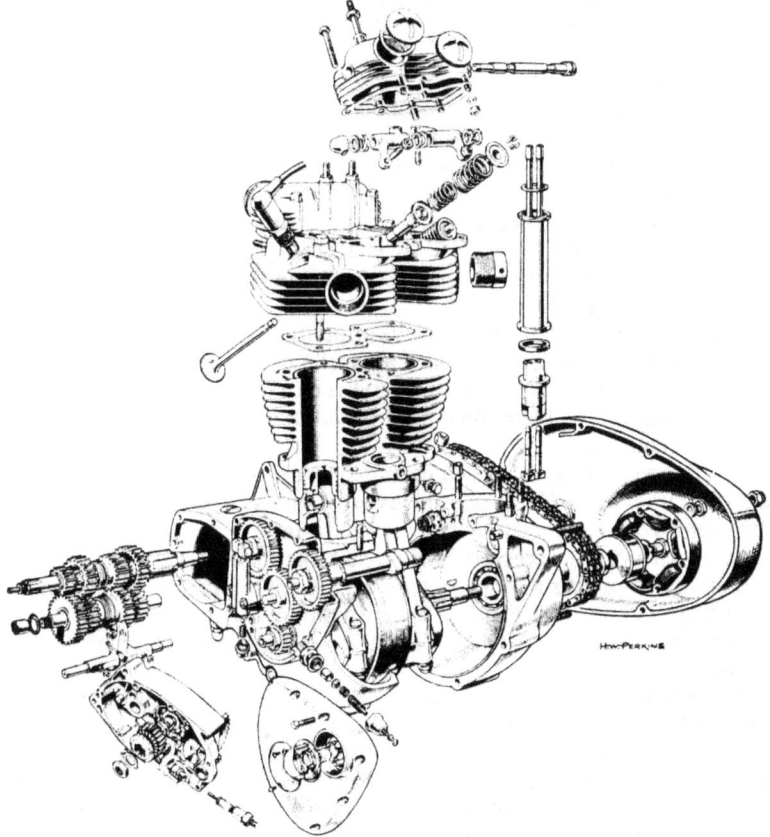

Fig. 56. Exploded view of unit-construction 350, 500 or 650 c.c. engine

The general design of the 1963 engine shown is, except for slight differences, the same for 1958–68 models 3TA, 5TA, T100A and T90, and T100S/S. Note, however, that on all 650 c.c. engines cupped ends of the push-rods engage ball ends of the tappets. The oil feed pipe to the overhead rocker-boxes, the kick-starter components and the foot gear-change mechanism are not shown. 1969 500 c.c. engines have a ball-journal main bearing for the crankshaft timing side; this enables the main oil supply to be fed directly into the timing side of the crankshaft instead of, as on earlier engines, through ducts drilled in the plain-bearing bush. All 1968–9 engines have tougher steel camshafts and Stellite-tipped inlet valve stems to ensure greater durability. Some other 1968–9 engine modifications are briefly referred to in the Preface

Testing: start up the engine, remove the oil tank filler cap (*see* Fig. 55) and place a finger over the hole in the return pipe for a few seconds to divert extra oil to the rocker gear. Run the engine for 5–10 minutes, allow it to cool, and check the nuts and bolts for tightness. Do not overtighten by using extra-long spanners. The leverage afforded by the spanners provided in the tool-kit is quite sufficient.

Removing Cylinder Head (All 1965–69 350 and 1965–7 500 c.c. Unit-Construction Models from Engine No. H 40528; and all 1963–69 650 c.c. Unit-construction Models from Engine No. DU 101). The following instructions should be observed—

Petrol Tank: first disconnect the leads from the battery terminals. Turn off both petrol taps and disconnect the petrol pipes after unscrewing their union nuts. Hold the unions with a spanner to prevent damage. Next raise the twinseat (*see* Fig. 55) and remove the tank support bolts.

On 1965–66 350 and 500 c.c. models after detaching the locking wire from the four bolts, unscrew and remove the latter. On 1967–9 350, 500 c.c. models, and 1963–69 650 c.c. machines, unscrew and remove the single rear bolt and after detaching the locking wire from the two front bolts, remove these bolts also.

Withdraw the petrol tank and its mounting rubbers at the front and rear. On all models provided with a nacelle top-unit, if the tank fouls the underside of the nacelle cover during a removal attempt, remove the two rear securing-screws from the latter in order to provide sufficient clearance for tank removal.

The Exhaust System: loosen each exhaust pipe finned-clip bolt and the silencer-clip bolt. Also loosen the exhaust pipe and silencer bracket nuts; then remove the complete exhaust system, tapping each pipe away from the exhaust port, if necessary, with a suitable mallet.

If your mount has a Siamese-type exhaust system it is necessary first to loosen the left-to-right exhaust-pipe junction clip, and then tap the R.H. exhaust pipe until it is freed. The L.H. exhaust pipe can then be withdrawn.

Ignition Coils and Cables: disconnect the h.t. cables and the wiring harness from the L.H. and R.H. ignition coils and remove the latter. To do this it is necessary to remove the top and bottom coil mounting-bolts and the distance-pieces. On 650 c.c. engines remove the two torque stays secured to the rocker-boxes by four nuts and by mounting bolts and distance-pieces at the front and rear.

Rocker Feed Pipe: unscrew the two domed nuts securing the oil feed pipe for the overhead rocker spindles. On 350 and 500 c.c. engines withdraw the centrally-mounted oil-feed bolts. Be careful not to bend the oil feed pipe excessively and thereby cause a fracture.

Rocker-boxes: remove all four rocker-box slotted inspection caps and their filter washers. Then unscrew the two nuts from the studs fitted to the underneath of the exhaust rocker-box. On 350 and 500 c.c. engines also remove the two Phillips screws from the top of each rocker-box, loosen all eight cylinder-head securing bolts (*see* Fig. 58) and remove the four central ones. On 650 c.c. engines remove the exhaust rocker-box two outer securing bolts and, as in the case of 350 and 500 c.c. engines, remove the four central cylinder-head bolts (*see* Fig. 59).

The exhaust rocker-box and its gasket are now free to be removed, and at this stage the rocker-box may rise slightly because of an exhaust valve

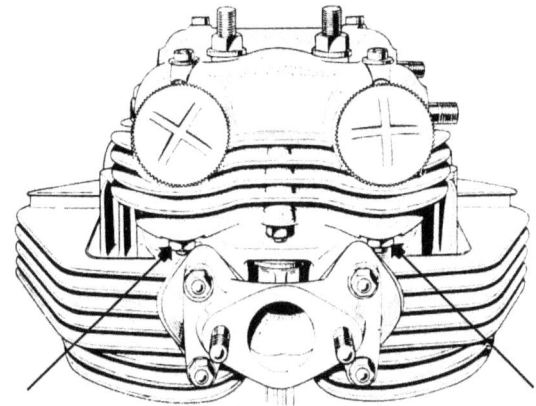

Fig. 57. On 1963–69 650 c.c. engines the two nuts shown arrowed may be rather difficult to remove

On the 350 and 500 c.c. unit-construction models the nuts indicated above are not so confined
(*From Triumph Workshop Manual*)

spring being compressed. Remove the inlet rocker-box similarly, but note that on 650 c.c. engines the nuts securing the inlet rocker-box shown arrowed in Fig. 57 may be rather difficult to remove because of the limited space between them and the top of the cylinder head. The remedy is to loosen these nuts slightly and then remove them later by lifting the rocker-box as required immediately prior to the actual removal of the rocker-box.

Be careful not to lose any of the six plain washers located beneath each of the underside rocker-box securing nuts. These washers are apt to adhere to the cylinder-head flanges.

Push-rods: after removing both rocker-boxes withdraw the four inlet and exhaust push-rods. Each must be subsequently replaced in its original position, and the four push-rods should therefore be laid aside in such a manner that each can be identified for position on the engine to ensure correct re-assembly. A 1969 push-rod cover tube is shown in Fig. 66.

Amal Carburettor: disconnect the air filter(s) if provided. If a *single* carburettor is fitted, this instrument should be completely removed or (if accessibility is poor) disconnected from the induction manifold by removing the carburettor-flange securing nuts and spring washers.

Where *two* carburettors are provided (as on Model T120), remove both carburettors from the cylinder head prior to head removal after removing the carburettor-flange securing nuts and spring washers. Position the carburettor(s) well clear of the cylinder head. Alternatively remove both carburettor(s) from the cylinder head and motor-cycle after withdrawing the throttle and air slides to which the control cables are attached.

The Cylinder Head: unscrew the remaining four cylinder-head securing bolts (five on 650 c.c. engines), a turn at a time (to maintain even pressure) and then carefully withdraw the cylinder head from the cylinder block. When doing this in the case of a few single-cylinder models where (because of poor accessibility) the carburettor has previously only been *disconnected* from the manifold, remove the instrument completely while simultaneously moving forward and withdrawing the cylinder head. Do *not* remove the induction manifold.

Finally, remove the two push-rod cover tubes. If their oil seals are worn or have in any way deteriorated, their renewal is called for prior to subsequent assembly.

To Replace Cylinder Head (All 1965–69 350 and 1965–7 500 c.c. Unit-construction Models from Engine No. H 40528; and all 1963–9 650 c.c. Unit-construction Models from Engine No. DU 101). Assemble the cylinder head as follows—

Gaskets: with a soft-metal scraper clean the faces for the two cylinder head/rocker-box joints and have available two *new* gaskets. The copper cylinder-head gasket should also either be renewed or reconditioned by heating it to a cherry red and plunging it into cold water. With some fine-grade emery cloth remove all scale from the cylinder head gasket prior to annealing it.

Cylinder Head and Rocker-boxes: grease the large gasket for the cylinder head and after thoroughly cleaning the head and cylinder block joint faces, carefully position the gasket on the block. When doing this make sure that the eight bolt holes (nine on 650 c.c. engines) are accurately aligned. Next locate the two push-rod cover tubes (complete with top and bottom oil seals) on the tappet guide-blocks. Then gently lower the cylinder head on to the cylinder block.

Replace and tighten finger-tight the four outer cylinder-head bolts and on 650 c.c. engines also fit and tighten the central bolt (*see* Figs. 58 and 59). Replace the four inlet and exhaust push-rods in their *original positions*, and then proceed to fit the two rocker-boxes. When fitting the push-rods, grease their bottom ends slightly and carefully position all four push-rods individually, making sure that their bottom cups or ball-ends (on 350 and 500 c.c. engines) fully engage the corresponding tappet ball-ends or cups respectively.

Slowly rotate the engine (with sparking plugs removed) until both *inlet* push-rods are level with each other and right down; then fit the *inlet* rocker-box and its new gasket to the cylinder head. When doing

GENERAL MAINTENANCE: THE ENGINE 109

this make quite sure that cupped upper ends of the four push-rods fully engage the ball-ended adjuster screws on the overhead rocker-arms.

On all engines replace the four central cylinder-head through bolts. Tighten these bolts finger-tight only. Then on 350 and 500 c.c. engines

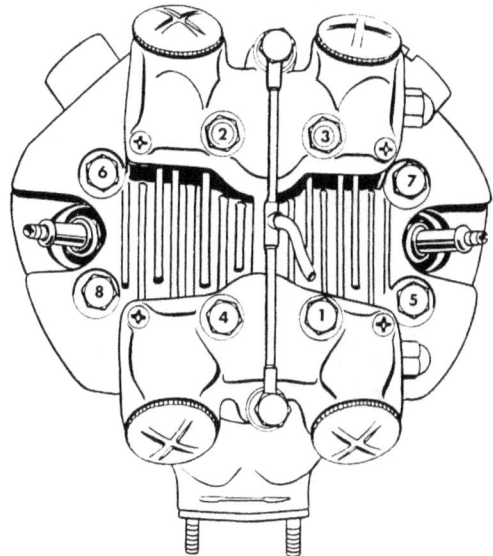

Fig. 58. Recommended tightening and loosening sequence for cylinder head and rocker-box securing bolts (350 c.c. and pre-1968 500 c.c. unit-construction models)

On all 1968–9 500 c.c. Triumph twins a different cylinder head, as fitted to the 500 c.c. Daytona model T100T, is provided. The removal and fitting of this head which has large-size inlet valves is dealt with as for 1967 500 c.c. engines.

screw the two outer Phillips screws into the top of the inlet rocker-box. Also replace and screw home two underside retaining nuts and plain washers (see Fig. 57). Assemble the exhaust rocker-box as just described for the inlet rocker-box. Before finally clamping down both rocker-boxes verify that the valves are functioning properly by slow engine rotation.

First tighten down firmly the four central bolts (double-ended bolts on 650 c.c. engines) which secure the cylinder head as well as the two rocker-boxes. Fully tighten the eight or nine cylinder-head securing bolts in the sequence shown in Fig. 58 or 59 according to whether your engine capacity is 350, 500 or 650 c.c. After finally tightening down the cylinder head and rocker-box assembly, adjust the valve clearances (see page 92) and tighten down securely the four rocker-box inspection caps, not omitting to replace their fibre washers. Replace both the sparking plugs after checking their gaps and cleaning them.

Rocker Oil Feed Pipe: connect up the oil feed pipe for the overhead rockers and rocker spindles. On 350 and 500 c.c. engines replace and tighten the centrally-mounted oil-feed bolts, and on all engines tighten firmly the two domed nuts which secure the pipe. When replacing the pipe be most careful not to bend it excessively, and fit new copper washers (or annealed old ones) over the ends of the rocker spindles.

Amal Carburettor: replace the carburettor(s) and see that the flange-securing nuts are evenly and firmly tightened, not omitting to replace the

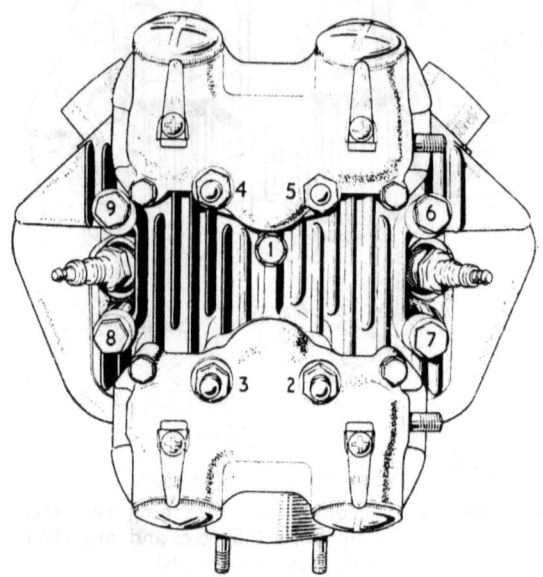

Fig. 59. Recommended tightening and loosening sequence for cylinder head, rocker-box securing bolts (pre-1968 650 c.c. unit-construction)
(*From Triumph Workshop Manual*)

spring washers. If the throttle and air slides were previously removed, replace them and check for their free movement in the mixing chamber(s). Finally reconnect the air filter(s), where provided (*see* page 20).

Torque Stays: replace the torque stay(s) and do not forget to replace the distance-pieces. On 350 and 500 c.c. engines tighten firmly the two nuts and the mounting bolt securing the single torque-stay, and on 650 c.c. engines tighten securely the four nuts and mounting bolts.

Ignition Coils and Cables: replace the twin ignition-coils and secure them with their top and bottom mounting bolts after replacing the distance-pieces. Reconnect the wiring harness correctly to the L.H. and R.H. ignition coils, and connect the h.t. leads to the correct sparking plugs.

The Exhaust System: replace both exhaust pipes and silencers and firmly secure the whole exhaust system by fully tightening the finned-clip

GENERAL MAINTENANCE: THE ENGINE

bolts and exhaust pipe and silencer bracket nuts. If a Siamese-type exhaust system is provided on your model, make sure that you tighten firmly the left-to-right pipe junction-clip after replacing the L.H. exhaust pipe. To make sure that a tight-fitting exhaust pipe does go right home into the exhaust port, it is advisable to give the curve of the pipe a few slight biffs with a mallet.

Petrol Tank: with the twinseat raised, position the tank-mounting rubbers and the petrol tank itself. Any damaged rubbers should be renewed. Screw home and tighten the four tank-support bolts (three provided on 650 c.c. models). Lock the four bolts (the two front bolts on 650 c.c. models) by re-threading the locking wire through their heads. If the two rear screws have previously been removed from a nacelle top-unit to facilitate tank removal, see that these screws are replaced and firmly tightened.

A Final Check: warm up your engine at normal tick-over speed and make a slow-running carburettor adjustment if necessary (*see* page 13). Allow your engine and yourself to cool off and then check all external nuts and bolts for tightness.

Removing the Carbon. Care and thoroughness in decarbonizing well repays the labour expended and, after all, you are preparing the engine for about another 10,000 miles' running without complaining!

On most 1956 and later engines the cylinder head as well as the pistons are made of *light alloy* and it is inadvisable to remove carbon deposits from their comparatively soft surfaces with a screwdriver or any other type of steel implement. Instead, use a blunt aluminium scraper (proprietary or home-made), or else a piece of lead solder flattened at one end. When removing carbon deposits from the cylinder-head combustion chambers *always* take great care not to damage the valve seats.

It is safest to keep the four valves temporarily in position prior to inspecting the seats and valve faces and grinding-in the valves if necessary. Remove all traces of carbon from the interior surfaces and do not forget the ports (especially the exhaust ports) and the sparking plug holes. Carbon forms less easily on a polished surface and it is a good plan to polish the combustion chamber surfaces of a cast-iron head with some fine emery cloth, but this should be done *before* the valves are removed, and afterwards all traces of abrasive must be cleaned away with a rag and paraffin. *On no account use emery cloth where an aluminium-alloy head is used.* Also take special care not to use excessive pressure with the scraper and thereby deeply scratch the combustion chamber walls.

The pistons are both made of a light-alloy and are therefore vulnerable to careless decarbonizing. Carefully clean away the carbon deposits from the piston crowns. When removing the carbon each piston should, of course, be placed at T.D.C. On no account use emery cloth or any abrasive to polish the piston crowns. If abrasive particles get past the top piston rings no end of damage may be caused to the cylinder bores.

Some novices are apt to overlook this vital point. If the pistons are not removed (rarely necessary) and the cylinder block is left undisturbed (normally recommended), do not remove the slight carbon ring deposits on the piston crown circumferences.* They form an excellent oil seal and can cause no harm, provided the deposits are not thick. As is the case with a light-alloy cylinder head, be particularly careful not to scratch the piston crowns deeply when chipping off the carbon. By holding the scraper at a suitable angle, using the right type of scraper, and not using excessive force, this can be avoided. After removing all traces of carbon, clean both piston crowns with a clean rag damped in paraffin, and cover up the mouths of the cylinder bores.

To Remove the Valves. As has already been mentioned on page 98, the valves should all be removed and inspected when decarbonizing. A

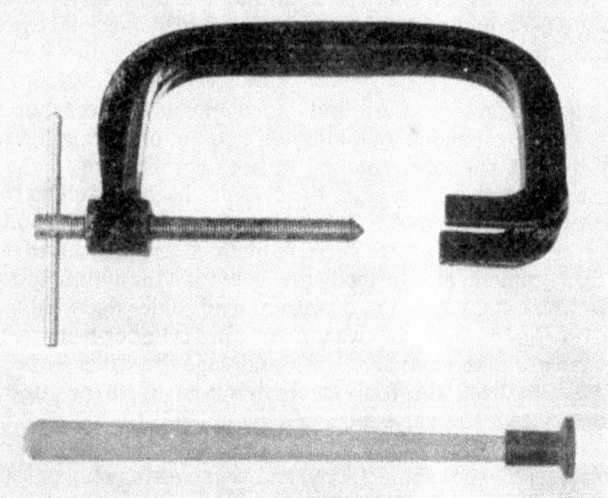

Fig. 60. Two useful proprietary tools for the valves

Above is shown a sturdy valve spring compressor, and below a suction type valve grinding tool

close examination of the valve seats should also be made. To remove the valves it is desirable to use a good valve spring compressor such as the tool shown in Fig. 60. It can be obtained from a Triumph dealer or an accessory firm. Compress the valve spring with the spring compressor, with the forked end of the tool contacting the valve spring top collar.

* It is also not advisable to disturb any slight carbon rings found inside and near the tops of the cylinder bores. To maintain the slight carbon rings referred to, when decarbonizing each piston crown it is a good plan to lay an old piston ring on the top of the piston when in the T.D.C. position.

GENERAL MAINTENANCE: THE ENGINE

After turning the tommy bar or wing nut of the compressor several turns, loosen the split collet by delivering a sharp tap with a hammer on the forked end of the tool. The split collet halves can then be eased away with a narrow screwdriver or similar tool. Release the valve spring compressor and withdraw the top collar, the inner and outer valve springs and the valve itself. Deal with each of the four valves similarly, and be careful not to mix up the valves. They must be replaced exactly as removed. The inlet and exhaust valves are marked "IN" and "EX" to assist correct replacement and should be marked for correct position by you.

Examining Valve Springs. After a considerable mileage the valve springs lose their tension, and their length decreases. If a new duplex spring is available, check the free length of each inner and outer spring with the corresponding lengths of the new duplex valve spring. If a valve spring is found unsatisfactory it is the best policy to replace all four duplex springs with a new set. They are not expensive, but are most important.

Insert each valve stem in its guide and check for play by attempting to move the valve sideways. If there is much wear and scuffing, replace the

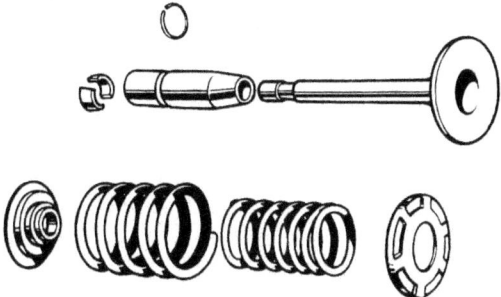

Fig. 61. Valve, valve guide and duplex-spring assembly shown dismantled (all engines)

On all 650 c.c. unit-construction engines the bottom cup for the duplex valve spring is of slightly different type, and the spring circlip for the valve guide is omitted

(From Triumph Workshop Manual)

valve. A new valve will, of course, require to be ground-in. A valve stem often wears more than its guide, and a distinct shoulder may be felt near the neck of the valve. In this case fitting a new valve will probably remedy slackness without fitting a new valve guide.

Grinding-in the Valves. Use the suction tool shown in Fig. 60 or alternatively a metal grinding-in tool which can be secured to the tip of the valve stems. To grind-in a valve (see that it is the correct one), holding the cylinder head firmly on a bench or table, clean both the valve seat and the valve face. Smear with a piece of rag or the finger tip a thin film of fine carborundum grinding paste (coarse at first if handling a valve seat and valve face which are badly pitted) on the bevelled valve face. Replace the valve in its guide minus the valve spring. Be careful not to interchange the inlet and exhaust valves (*see* page 113).

When grinding-in a valve, a light pressure on the grinding tool is required and care must be taken not to rock the valve, particularly if the valve guide is slightly worn. Rotate the valve about a *third of a turn* in one direction and then an equal amount in the opposite direction, pausing every few oscillations to raise the valve from its seat and turn about 180 degrees. Cease grinding-in when no "cut" can be felt (and the valve begins to "sing") and put some more grinding paste on the bevelled edge of the valve face if, after cleaning the valve in paraffin, some pitting is still visible.

Proceed with grinding-in until both the valve bevelled face and seat have a matt metallic surface uniformly over an appreciable width (line contact is not sufficient) and there are no pitting marks left on the valve or its seating after wiping the paste off.* Note that excessive grinding-in after a good seating has been effected, or in any circumstances, can lead to the valve becoming "pocketed" which causes an appreciable decline in the power output of the engine. Always take a cylinder head with very badly pitted valve seats to a Triumph dealer for valve seat refacing. Before making a final examination of the valve and its seating, thoroughly clean them both with a paraffin- or petrol-soaked rag to ensure that there is no trace of abrasive left. Afterwards put the rag in the dustbin.

Refitting the Valves. After grinding-in the valves, assemble them in their initial positions in the cylinder head. Valve stem end-caps are not provided. See that all parts are quite clean, and fit each valve in the following manner. Smear the valve stem with some engine oil and insert the valve stem in its guide and, holding the valve head against its seat, turn the cylinder head on its side, replace the lower spring cup over the valve guide, next the duplex valve spring, and finally the outer collar. Now, with the valve spring compressor, compress the valve spring until the split collet can be fitted into the outer collar and around the valve stem groove. Make sure that the collet beds down properly. The application of a little grease to the inside of a split collet helps it to stick on the valve stem until the duplex spring is released by removing the pressure exerted by the valve spring compressor tool. After releasing the tool, tap the stem head of the valve smartly to ensure correct bedding down of the split collet.

* A recommended and highly efficient method of checking that there is a perfect and uniform seal between a valve face and its cylinder-head seat is to remove all grinding paste, clean the contacting surfaces with paraffin and then apply a smear of "Engineer's" marking blue to the valve seat. One complete valve turn should leave an unbroken ring of marking blue on the valve seat.

GENERAL MAINTENANCE: THE ENGINE

Removing the Cylinder Block (All Engines). Where cylinder block removal is necessary (not often advised), unscrew the eight nuts which hold it to the crankcase studs. Also secure the tappets in the cylinder block by pressing a rubber wedge between the tappets (*see* Fig. 65). With both of the pistons positioned at T.D.C., gently lift the cylinder block off the two pistons. Before removing the block completely it is a good plan to raise the block some distance and then place a clean cloth over the mouth of the crankcase. This will prevent any dirt or piece of broken piston ring (or a tappet acidentally freed) entering the crankcase. It is extremely difficult to extract dirt or pieces of metal from the crankcase. When the cylinder block is removed test the connecting-rods for vertical play at B.D.C.

After removing the cylinder block and its washer or gasket (which should be renewed unless perfect) from the crankcase face, do not without good reason remove the *rubber wedge* previously inserted between each pair of tappets. If the tappets are accidentally or deliberately removed, it is important to be able subsequently to identify each *individual* tappet to ensure its later replacement in its original position in its original tappet guide block. Any interchange is liable to cause excessive tappet and cam wear and also reduce engine efficiency.

Examining and Removing the Piston Rings. The piston rings are responsible for maintaining good compression. They must therefore be full of spring, free in their grooves, and set with their gaps opposite to each other (i.e., at 120 degrees in the case of the three-ring pistons provided on the twin-cylinder engines). If all three rings are bright all the way round, they are obviously being nicely polished and satisfactorily contact the cylinder bores, and should be left alone. If the rings are discoloured at some points they are not making good contact with the bores, thereby causing gas to blow past them. Possibly some rings are stuck in their grooves with burnt oil and will function correctly if the piston ring grooves are cleaned. Should the rings be scored, are vertically loose in their grooves, or have lost their proper tension and gap, renewal of the rings concerned should be effected.

Piston rings are made of cast-iron and are small in section. They must therefore always be handled with extreme care. The bottom ring on each piston is a scraper ring and this is particularly vulnerable to damage. Piston rings cannot safely be opened out wider than will enable them to slip over the crowns of the pistons. Excessively wide opening out of any piston ring will cause it to snap immediately. To remove or replace used rings, or fit new piston rings, it is best to insert small strips of sheet-metal (about $\frac{3}{8}$ in. wide and 2 in. long) in the manner shown in Fig. 62. Be careful to note the order in which piston rings are removed so as to ensure their being correctly replaced. When fitting piston rings, thoroughly clean the grooves into which they fit, as any deposit left at the back of new rings forces them out and makes them too tight a fit. Paraffin will usually loosen stuck rings.

When renewing the piston rings, always fit rings supplied by a Triumph dealer or a firm handling Triumph spares. Piston rings are made to extremely fine limits. It is particularly important to note that on all

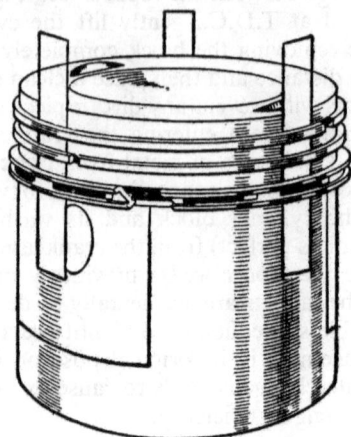

Fig. 62. A safe method of removing and fitting piston rings

Note the slotted scraper ring below the two compression rings. This ring is very fragile. Some rings are marked on one face "TOP" (see text)

engines the second compression ring (i.e. the centre ring) has the word "TOP" etched on one face as shown in Fig. 63. This ring must always face *towards the piston crown*. The face is tapered, hence the importance of the ring being correctly fitted on all 1956–69 engines.

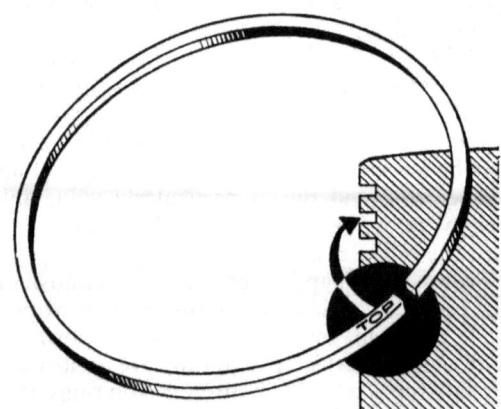

Fig. 63. Where only one taper-faced piston ring is provided, it must always be fitted like this

GENERAL MAINTENANCE: THE ENGINE

On all late 1963-69 350, 500 and 650 c.c. unit-construction engines *both* compression rings have tapered faces marked "TOP" and all rings except bottom (slotted) scraper rings must therefore be fitted as indicated in Fig. 63.

Before fitting used piston rings do not forget to scrape off all carbon from the backs of the rings and from the ends of the rings. Also clean out the oil drain holes in the scraper-ring grooves. To clean the piston ring grooves it is a good plan to use an old broken ring and insert the broken end into the groove and work it round the circumference.

Checking the Gap of New Piston Rings. Before fitting a new piston ring, check its gap in the lowest part of the cylinder block bore. For checking purposes the piston ring should lie square to the bore. To ensure this, place the bottom of the piston skirt on to the ring and ease it about $\frac{1}{2}$ in. down the bore. With a feeler gauge check the gap.

Correct Ring Gaps. The correct gap for the two compression rings (new) on all 1956-62 500 and 650 c.c. pre-unit construction models is 0·010 in.–0·014 in. For the same engines the correct gap for the single scraper ring (new) is 0·007 in.–0·010 in.

On all 1958-69 350 c.c. unit-construction models the correct gap for the two compression rings and single scraper ring (new) is 0·008 in.–0·011 in. In the case of all 1958-69 500 and 650 c.c. unit-construction models the correct gap for the two compression rings and single scraper ring (new) is 0·010 in.–0·014 in.

Incorrect Clearances. Never fit new piston rings with insufficient gaps or side clearance in the piston grooves. The gap of a new compression or scraper ring if found less than the minimum recommended gap referred to above, should be increased as required by clamping the ring between two wooden blocks in a vice and very carefully filing one of its diagonal ends. As regards excessive ring gap, it is advisable to fit new piston rings when the gap of used rings exceeds the recommended maximum gap for new rings by 0·005 in.–0·006 in.

If a new piston ring has insufficient vertical side-clearance in the corresponding piston groove, rub down one side of the ring (not that marked "TOP") on a sheet of fine carborundum paper, laid on a piece of plate glass or other dead smooth surface, using a semi-rotary motion. Continue until the ring is a free fit in its piston groove, with minimum clearance.

Oversize Pistons and Rings. An increase in the diameter of the upper part of the cylinder bore through wear exceeding 0·005 in. (0·13 mm) indicates that a rebore by a competent engineering firm is necessary. Pistons 0·010 in., 0·020 in., 0·030 in. and 0·040 in. oversize to suit are obtainable from the Triumph Engineering Co. Ltd.

Removing the Pistons (All Engines). Piston removal is seldom necessary or advisable. The following is the procedure to use for removing each piston. Remove both circlips from the piston bosses after first checking that the mouth of the crankcase is completely covered with a cloth. Each circlip must be renewed after removal. This is important. To remove each

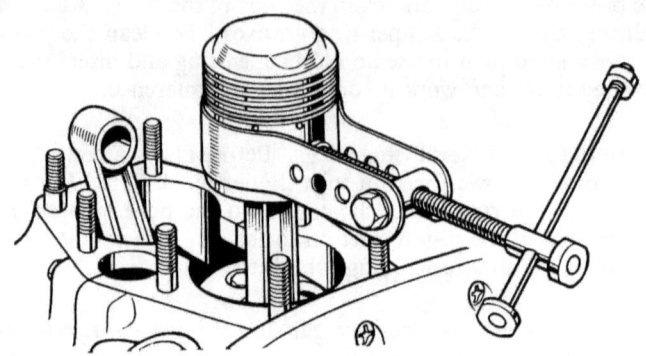

Fig. 64. Using a proprietary tool for pressing the gudgeon-pin in or out of a piston

The type of tool shown (a Terry) has three alternative pressure pads to suit different diameter gudgeon-pins and is suitable for all 1956–69 350, 500 and 650 c.c. Triumph engines. Alternatively use the Triumph service tool Z72 or warm the piston and use a suitable drift

(From Triumph Workshop Manual)

circlip, use a small screwdriver or a pointed instrument such as the tang end of a file.

The gudgeon-pin is a fairly tight fit in the piston bosses (especially on a new engine). After removing both circlips use a proprietary tool such as that shown in Fig. 64 for pressing out the gudgeon-pin. Alternatively use a suitable diameter drift and light hammer to knock out the pin. If this method is used it is essential to support the piston firmly on the side opposite that where the hammer is applied. Failure to provide good support can cause an excessive side-stress to be imposed on the connecting-rod. Should any difficulty be experienced in removing a gudgeon-pin, warm the piston by wrapping a cloth round the piston after immersing the cloth in hot water and wringing it out. This also applies to replacing pistons as described in the next paragraph. To ensure their replacement (essential) in their original positions on their original connecting-rods, scribe in the appropriate position inside each piston the abbreviation "LF" or "RF."

Replacing the Pistons. When replacing a piston see that you fit it to the correct connecting-rod the right way round. Oil the small-end bush of the connecting-rod and position the piston with one *new* circlip fitted. From the opposite side press or tap the gudgeon-pin (which should also be oiled)

GENERAL MAINTENANCE: THE ENGINE 119

home until its end abuts the circlip already fitted. Then fit the remaining *new* circlip. Make sure that both circlips are fully bedded down in the piston grooves. Lubricate the piston rings and position the rings so that their gaps are correctly positioned (*see* page 115).

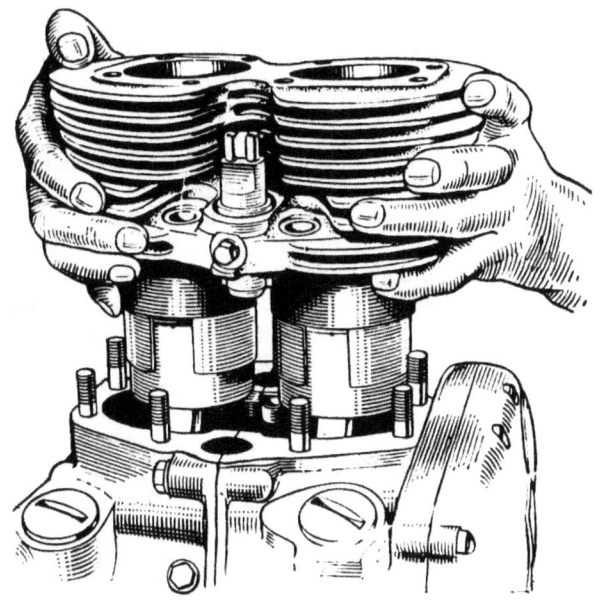

Fig. 65. Lowering the cylinder block over the two pistons

Note the rubber wedge inserted between the tappets to prevent the tappets falling into the crankcase. Also note the two clips fitted around the piston rings

(Triumph Engineering Co., Ltd.)

Re-fitting the Cylinder Block. Grease the washer for the cylinder block face. If not perfect, fit a new washer. It is assumed that both pistons are near B.D.C. and that the inlet and exhaust tappets are in position in the tappet blocks. Place a rubber wedge (*see* Fig. 65) between each pair of tappet stems to prevent the tappets falling into the crankcase when fitting the cylinder block. Oil both cylinder block bores thoroughly, especially at their upper ends and then carefully lower the cylinder block over the pistons, which should have piston ring clips fitted as shown in Fig. 65, until the piston rings slide up into the two cylinder block bores.

While holding the cylinder block squarely, get an assistant to turn the engine over slowly so as to slide the two pistons up into the cylinder block bores. As the pistons enter the bores, the piston ring clips will fall clear and can be withdrawn over the connecting-rods. Guide the cylinder block over the crankcase studs and then remove the rubber wedges from the two pairs of tappets. Replace the eight spring washers and nuts securing the cylinder block to the crankcase studs, and tighten the nuts firmly and in a diagonal order. Tighten them all finger-tight first.

In conclusion, here are two important points to remember during final assembly: (*a*) when you lower the cylinder block on the crankcase face always make quite sure that it is properly located over the two crankcase dowels; (*b*) when securing the cylinder block of a 650 c.c. unit-construction engine, see that the four *smaller* nuts are fitted to the four *central* crankcase studs.

Spares and Repairs. The author would emphasize that the contents of this handbook do *not* include detailed instructions for complete stripping-down and *major overhaul*, work which necessarily requires some workshop facilities, special Triumph Service Tools and considerable mechanical knowledge and aptitude. If, however, you have suitable facilities, skill and time to undertake such work, you are strongly advised first to refer to the detailed procedure described in the appropriate *Triumph Workshop Manual*. These are three excellent publications any of which can be obtained from your nearest Triumph spares dealer (not from the makers). If in any doubt about your ability to tackle a major overhaul job, get this done by the Triumph Service Department or by a firm specializing in Triumph overhaul and repairs.

Some useful addresses can often be obtained by perusing the Classified Advertisement pages of *Motor Cycle*, a weekly paper published at 1s. This paper also has a technical queries Dept. at its offices in Dorset House, Stamford Street, London, S.E.1. A stamped, addressed envelope must be enclosed for reply.

In the U.K. there are now over 200 established dealers holdings comprehensive stocks of genuine Triumph spares, and an up-to-date list of them can be obtained by return on application to The Triumph Engineering Co. Limited, Meriden Works, Allesley, Coventry (Phone: 067/62/3331).

Appendix: General Maintenance

(1968–9 Models T90, T100S/S, TR6, T120)

THIS appendix covers general maintenance required for the above-mentioned Triumph twins, other than appropriate instructions already included for those models in the preceding six chapters. Most of the basic 1968–9 Triumph modifications have already been outlined in the Preface and it remains to deal with the maintenance aspect of those modifications not already covered in this handbook.

THE ENGINE

Lubrication. On all three 1969 models the oil tank filler-cap has an integral dipstick; maintain as far as possible the contents of the tank at the level indicated "Full" on this dipstick.

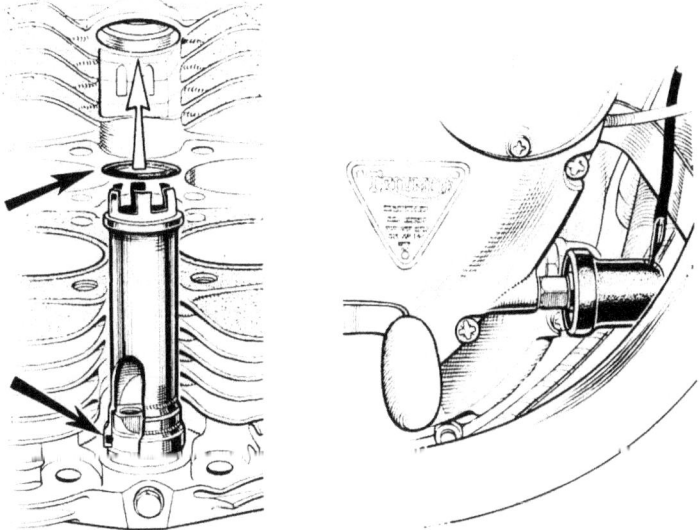

Figs. 66, 67. Two new features in the 1969 lubrication system

All 1969 models have oil seals (shown arrowed) for each push-rod cover tube, and a switch (shown right) at the front of the timing case regulates a red oil-pressure warning light in the shell of the Lucas headlamp

(By courtesy of "Motor Cycle"—London)

To minimize the risk of oil leakage from the push-rod cover tubes, on the 1969 engines each of the two-piece telescopic cover-tubes has two oil seals (Fig. 66). The upper joint is made a sliding fit to allow for cylinder and cylinder-head expansion when warming up the engine. After covering a considerable mileage renew the two oil seals if they show signs of deterioration.

A major modification featured in the 1969 lubrication system is a red oil-pressure warning light (with Lucas 281 bulb), illustrated in Fig. 71; its actuating switch is located on the offside at the front of the timing case as shown in Fig. 67. Always keep the oil pressure well above 7 lb. per sq. in. which is the danger limit (*see* page 29).

Lubricate the Lucas type 6CA contact-breaker and centrifugal automatic-advance mechanism every 3,000 miles as described on page 126.

The Amal "Concentric" Carburettor(s). The "concentric", Series 600 or 900, fitted (singly or in pairs) to all 1968-9 Triumph twins, differs appreciably in detail design and layout from the "monobloc" instrument fitted to most pre-1968 models. Its *basic* design, functioning and maintenance are, however, very similar in both instances.

As may be observed by comparing Figs. 4 and 68, the primary design modifications are the provision of a *detachable* and *vertical* float-chamber with top petrol feed, and the use of a different pilot-jet layout. Because the float-chamber is vertical, jet removal is impossible without first removing the float-chamber unit.

Tuning "Concentric" Carburettor(s). The general advice given on pages 12-16 for the Amal "monobloc" instrument applies also to the Series 600 or 900 "concentric" instrument provided on the 1968-9 Triumph twin range, except in regard to minor differences necessitated by the above-mentioned design modifications. Maintenance and tuning are little affected.

Never, except for very special reasons, alter the maker's carburettor settings given in the accompanying table. Confine your tuning, *where*

AMAL CARBURETTOR SETTINGS FOR 1968-9 MODELS

Triumph Model	Main Jet Size	Throttle Valve	Needle Position
T90 (348 c.c.)	140	3½	2
T100S (490 c.c.)	190	3½	2
TR6 (649 c.c.)	230	4	Middle
T120 (649 c.c.)	220	3	Middle

necessary, to effecting a good slow-running adjustment by making a combined adjustment of the pilot air-adjusting screw and the throttle-stop, using the general procedure described on page 13. If a thorough slow-running adjustment does not effect a smooth tick-over at moderate speed, consider one or more of the possible causes suggested on page 15.

APPENDIX: GENERAL MAINTENANCE   123

The final test of a perfect slow-running adjustment is to "rev" the engine up and down sharply several times with the machine stationary and also while riding with *first* gear engaged. If the adjustment is perfect, the exhaust note should be nice and crisp and there should be no "flat spots" or "spitting back" when the throttle twist-grip is sharply turned. Acceleration should be quick and smooth. If twin carburettors are provided (e.g. on model T120), some synchronizing may be required

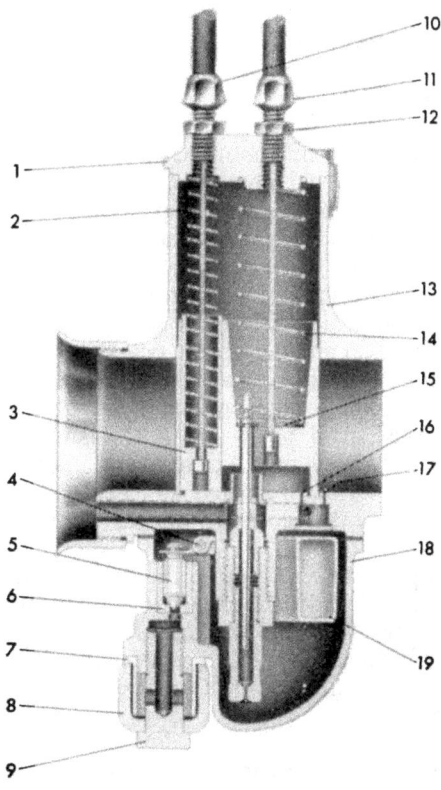

Fig. 68. Sectional view through mixing chamber and float chamber of Amal "Concentric" carburettor (Series 600 or 900)

Key

1. Mixing chamber cap
2. Return spring for 3
3. Air valve
4. Float spindle
5. Float-chamber needle
6. Seating for 5
7. Filter gauze
8. Banjo
9. Securing bolt for 8
10. Cable adjuster (air valve)
11. Cable adjuster (throttle valve)
12. Lock-nut for 11
13. Mixing-chamber
14. Return spring for throttle valve
15. Jet-needle spring clip
16. Pilot by-pass
17. Pilot outlet
18. Float chamber (vertical and detachable)
19. Float for 18

(*see* page 14) to ensure that both the throttle valves have a simultaneous and identical movement in their mixing chambers.

Dismantling "Concentric" Carburettor(s). Carburettor removal from the engine in the case of a "concentric" instrument differs little from "monobloc" carburettor removal (*see* page 16) except that the petrol feed-pipe banjo securing bolt is located as shown at (9) in Fig. 68, and it is necessary to remove two screws in order to detach the mixing-chamber cap (1).

Dismantling a "concentric" Series 600 or 900 Amal carburettor also differs only in minor detail from the procedure required for a "monobloc" instrument. A most useful Service tool can be obtained from any Amal spares stockist for a few shillings. This tool has a box spanner and tommy-bar for main jet removal; the tommy-bar has cross-slot screwdriver ends, one being angled for float chamber removal.

First remove the mixing-chamber cap (secured by two screws) and withdraw the throttle and air slides (valves) from the mixing chamber shown at (13) in Fig. 68. Then remove the spring clip (15) securing the tapered jet-needle to the throttle slide, compress the latter's return spring (14), and slide the cable nipple from the base of the air slide (3).

To remove the vertical and detachable type float chamber (18) from the body of the carburettor, unscrew and remove the two cross-slot screws and withdraw the complete unit which houses the hinged concentric float (19), its forked arm, pivot and float-chamber needle (5). After removing the float-chamber unit the main and pilot jets can, if desired, be removed forthwith. The former has no jet cover-nut as on the "monobloc" instrument. The main-jet holder and the needle jet can now also be removed.

Note that it is preferable to remove the main jet with the previously-mentioned Service tool and to remove the pilot jet by means of a small electrical screwdriver. Also note that rubber "O" rings are provided for the carburettor attachment flange and also for the shanks of the throttle-stop and pilot air-adjusting screws. Complete dismantling should prove quite straightforward.

Inspecting "Concentric" Carburettor Components. Observe the general advice given on pages 18–19 for the "monobloc" instrument.

Assembling "Concentric" Carburettor(s). Assemble a carburettor (*see* Fig. 68) in the reverse order of dismantling. When doing this note the following points. Do not again use any paper, fibre or rubber washers unless such washers are found to be in *perfect* condition.

When replacing the throttle valve in the carburettor mixing-chamber make sure that the jet needle engages properly with the needle jet. Make quite certain that the lower end of the jet needle actually enters the jet tube; also that the spring clip engages the correct jet-needle groove (*see*

APPENDIX: GENERAL MAINTENANCE 125

table on page 122) and that this clip lies flat against the inside base of the throttle valve.

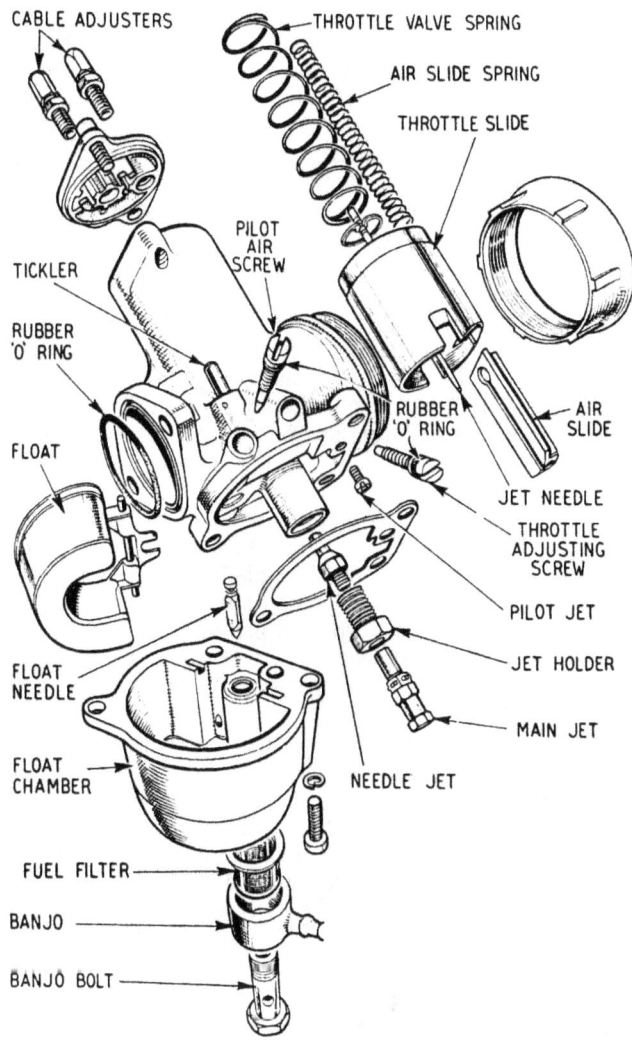

Fig. 69. Exploded view of Amal "Concenrtic" carburettor
(By Courtesy of B.S.A. Motor Cycles Ltd)

Note that with the latest horse-shoe shaped spring clip used to secure the jet needle to the throttle valve it is possible to connect the cable nipple socket in the throttle valve and then hold up the spring clip with the fingers and slip the jet needle into position with the needle-clip attached. Then release the spring to ensure that its lower end is holding the needle-clip flat against the inside base of the throttle valve.

When replacing the detachable float-chamber (*see* Fig. 68) check that the ends of the float hinge-pin are properly seated in their sockets and not partly resting on the flange face. If the end of a hinge-pin stands proud of its socket and rests on the flange, severe subsequent flooding is likely and the carburettor body and/or float-chamber may become damaged.

Also see that the extension of the float grips the neck of the float needle properly. Be careful to fit the float-chamber gasket the right way round to ensure correct alignment of its two rear holes with the jet passages in the float-chamber casting. Faulty replacement of this gasket is likely to cause some flooding.

When attaching a "concentric" carburettor to the induction manifold of a Triumph twin make sure that a new "O" ring is pressed fully home into the flange groove all round and that it does not overlap anywhere. After fitting the carburettor-flange gasket and positioning the carburettor flange over the manifold securing studs, tighten down absolutely evenly the flange securing nuts.

Contact-breaker Maintenance (Lucas Type 6CA). The type 6CA contact-breaker unit fitted to all 1968–9 350, 500, 650 c.c. Triumph twins is housed behind the circular chromium-plated cover secured by two screws to the timing-case cover. Details of the exhaust-camshaft driven unit which, of course, has two separate pairs of contacts are shown in Fig. 70. The maintenance required comprises: occasionally checking the gaps between the contacts, cleaning the contacts when necessary, and some minor lubrication.

Some initial settling-down of the nylon heels of the moving contacts occurs and it is therefore necessary to check both contact-breaker gaps after covering 500 miles on a new machine or one having a new or reconditioned contact-breaker unit. Subsequently check the gaps about every 3,000 miles. After checking the gaps, and also at regular intervals of about 3,000 miles, apply three drops of engine oil (*see* page 26) to each lubricating wick. These wicks are initially lubricated by the makers with Shell Retinax A.

To check the contact-breaker gaps, rotate the engine slowly forward, using the kick-starter, until the scribe mark on the operating cam aligns with the nylon heel of one pair of contacts. Then with appropriate feeler gauges check the gap which should be 0·015 in. If the gap is found to be outside the limits 0·014 in.–0·016 in., slacken the slotted nut which secures the stationary contact and move the contact until the gap is found to be correct; afterwards tighten the slotted nut. Now further rotate the engine forward until the second pair of contacts just begin to open and adjust the gap similarly.

APPENDIX: GENERAL MAINTENANCE 127

Inspect the contact-breaker contacts about every 3,000 miles and closely examine them for signs of burning and/or pitting. Clean the contacts with very fine emery cloth after removing them from their base

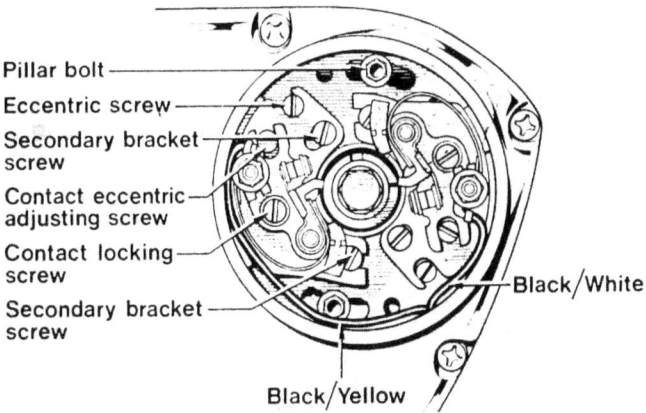

Fig. 70. Showing details of Lucas type 6CA contact-breaker unit
This unit supersedes the Lucas type 4CA unit fitted prior to 1968 and shown in Fig. 28
(Triumph Engineering Co. Ltd.)

plate. During their replacement make quite sure that all the insulating washers are correctly repositioned. Carefully adjust and check the gap between the contacts and then deal with the second pair of contacts in a similar manner.

When cleaning the contacts and adjusting their gaps place a few drops of clean engine oil (*see* page 26) on the centrifugal automatic-advance mechanism, also one or two drops on the felt pad responsible for cam lubrication. To minimize the risk of corrosion it is advisable also to apply two drops of engine oil to the spindle which supports the cam. A final word: be most careful *never* to allow any oil to get on the four contacts of the contact-breaker.

Contact-breaker Removal. If occasion is had to remove the contact-breaker unit shown in Fig. 70 it is necessary to remove the central bolt securing the unit to the exhaust camshaft and then to extract the unit using extractor tool D782 screwed into the end of the hollow spindle.

During the replacement of the contact-breaker unit it is essential to locate it correctly relative to the exhaust camshaft. The latter is provided with a pin, and a slot in the tapered end of the auto-advance spindle acts as a location.

Setting the Ignition Timing. On all 1968–9 350, 500, 650 c.c. engines the ignition timing is correctly set when the contacts of the contact-breaker commence to open with the crankshaft crank positioned 38 *degrees before top-dead-centre* (T.D.C.) and the contact-breaker in the *fully advanced* position.

For timing purposes two alternative methods have been provided for setting the engine in the 38 degrees fully advanced position. The first method utilizes service tools D653 and D654. By rotating the engine forward gently with the service tool fitted in place of the blanking plug at the top rear of the crankcase, slight hand pressure on the plunger will enable this to locate with a slot cut in the flywheel for this purpose.

On later engines the flywheel has *two* slots; one indicates T.D.C. and the other 38 degrees before T.D.C. When setting the timing as just referred to, check with a sparking plug removed that the pistons are not at T.D.C., otherwise the wrong slot in the flywheel is being used. The T.D.C. plug is for degree plate use only.

The second ignition setting method necessitates removal of the circular plate at the forward end of the oil-bath primary chaincase. Through the aperture you can observe the timing marking on the rotor casting and this aligns with a pointer on the chaincase at the edge of the aperture (on later machines). Positioning the rotor marking in line with the pointer again gives the 38 degree timing position.

To facilitate engine rotation, remove both sparking plugs. Adjust both pairs of contacts so that their gaps are correct (*see* page 65). Now set the engine at 38 degrees B.T.D.C. with the contact-breaker unit turned *clockwise* to the fully advanced position.

Check the left-hand contacts (black and yellow lead) which should be just beginning to open. If they are not, loosen both the pillar bolts (*see* Fig. 70) and turn the contact-breaker main back-plate. Turn clockwise if the contacts open too early and vice versa. When correct, lock up the back-plate, remove the flywheel locating plunger, if used, and rotate the engine over slowly through 360 degrees, i.e. one complete revolution.

Again set the engine at 38 degrees B.T.D.C., check that the cam is still in the fully advanced position, and then check that the second pair of contacts (black and white lead) is just commencing to open. Should some discrepancy exist, slacken the secondary back-plate top and bottom screws (*see* Fig. 70) and with the eccentric adjuster screw move the back-plate as required to obtain the correct point of opening.

Decarbonizing and Valve Grinding. The instructions given on pages 106–120 for 1965–67 models apply also to the corresponding 1968–69 unit-construction models except for a few very minor differences. The 1968–9 500 c.c. engines all have a slightly modified cylinder head with larger inlet valves; this head is similar to that provided on Model T100T (not covered in this handbook), but the procedure for removing and fitting this head (including the correct sequence for tightening the securing bolts) is exactly the same as for the other 1967 500 c.c. engines.

APPENDIX: GENERAL MAINTENANCE 129

THE MOTOR-CYCLE

The 1968-9 Control Layout. A nacelle is omitted on all 1968-9 Triumph twins, a separate Lucas headlamp bracketed to the front forks replacing the combined nacelle/headlamp unit. As may be observed in Fig. 71, the lighting and ignition switches have been transferred to the top of the headlamp shell and the near-side headlamp mounting bracket respectively.

The Lighting and Ignition Switches. The three-position lighting switch, hitherto of the rotary type, is on 1968-9 models a toggle-type Lucas No. 575A. This later switch has no markings. From the "OFF" position (on the left) move the toggle lever right to the first notch to switch the parking

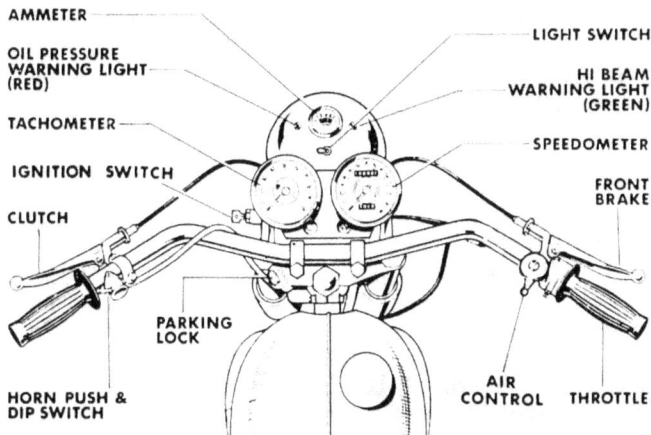

Fig. 71. The handlebar control layout on all 1968-9 models showing the new lighting and ignition switch positions

The steering damper, provided on many models, is not shown. A tachometer (r.p.m. indicator) is not standard equipment on the smaller capacity models, but is obtainable as an extra

lights on and further to the second notch to obtain full illumination from the headlamp. If a switch fault is suspected, test that the switch itself is at fault by substituting a new switch.

The ignition switch on the near-side headlamp bracket is operated by a key. To switch on the ignition, turn the key *clockwise*. Make a written note of the ignition switch and parking-lock key serial numbers in case you should accidentally lose either of these two important keys. The new Lucas type S45 ignition switch incorporates no emergency start position and the engine will start up with the igniton switched on even if the battery is "flat". The warning light remains on so long as the ignition is switched on, irrespective of whether the engine is running or not. It will remind you to switch off the ignition when leaving the machine with the engine stopped, and thereby prevent any unnecessary and wasteful discharge from the battery.

Other Items of Electrical Equipment. The alternator is a Lucas type RM19. This was fitted prior to 1968 (*see* page 47). The rectifier and Zener diode are also unchanged and the brief maintenance advice given on pages 56 and 57 respectively applies to the 1968–9 equipment.

Batteries provided on all 1968–9 Triumph twins are 12-volt Lucas units, type PUZ5A, and for maintenance instructions refer to the appropriate paragraphs on pages 61–63. Lucas type MA12 twin ignition coils supply the H.T. current. The minor maintenance required is outlined on page 57. Resistance H.T. cables are fitted as standard to eliminate the need for fitting supressors. Because of their design these cables *must* be replaced complete with terminal ends as a unit when renewal is required.

Stop-light Switches. All 1968–9 models have stop-light switches embodied on the front-brake cable. On 1969 650 c.c. models the rear-brake also has a stop-light switch incorporated on the secondary chain guard and actuated by the rear brake rod. In both cases the stop-light switches are sealed units, but the rear-brake switch can be adjusted as required.

Brake Adjustment. The instructions given on pages 76–77 apply to all 1968–9 models. Note, however, that a twin-leading shoe front brake is provided on all 1968 650 c.c. models and on all 1969 350, 500 and 650 c.c. Triumph twins. Some occasional adjustment of the external linkage rod becomes necessary.

Triumph Telescopic Front Forks. Shuttle-valve damping is included in the slightly modified 1968–9 fork assembly, but the maintenance instructions (*see* page 69) for pre-1968 front forks are not affected by the new modifications.

Steering Head Adjustment. This is not affected by the slightly modified telescopic front forks. For appropriate instructions refer to pages 70–72.

Wheel Removal and Fitting. Instructions applicable to 1968–9 front wheels are those given on page 72 for the 1956–67 models. Those applicable to the 1968–9 quickly-detachable rear wheels are as described on pages 75–76 for the 1963–7 Q.D. wheels.

Index

AIR—
  control lever, 1, 12
  filter, 20-2
  valve, inspecting, 18
Alternator, 47-8, 55
Ammeter, 4, 43, 44

BATTERY maintenance, 61-4
Brake—
  adjustment, 76, 180
  lubrication, 39
  pedal, 5, 77
  shoes, centralizing, 72
Brushgear, dynamo, 44
Bulbs, lamp, 58-61

CABLE connexions, battery, 63
Cables, high-tension, removing, 47, 53
Carburettor—
  Amal, 10-20, 122-6
  assembling, 19
  dismantling, 16-8
  flange, 18
  jet block, 18
  jet-needle clip, 18
  needle-jet, 18
  settings, 12, 14, 122
  S.U., 23
  tuning, 12-16
  working of, 10-12
Chain—
  adjustment, 78-80
  lubrication, 35-9
Cleaning—
  carburettor, 18
  chains, 80
  chromium, 69
  contact-breaker contacts, 55
  crankcase filter, 30
  distributor, 50
  enamel, 68
  engine and gearbox, 68
  magneto contacts, 46
  sparking plugs, 66
Clutch—
  adjustment, 84
  lubrication, 35
  plates and springs, 86, 88
Commutator, dynamo, 44

Contact-breaker—
  gaps, 51-4, 126
  lubrication, 50, 51
  magneto, 46
Control layout, 1-6, 129
Cylinder-block—
  removing, 115
  replacing, 119
Cylinder-head—
  removing, 99-109
  replacing, 100, 104, 108

DECARBONIZING, 98-111
Distributor, cleaning, 50
Dry sump system, 24
Dynamo output control, 43

EMERGENCY starting, 8, 47, 54
Enamel, cleaning, 68
Energy-transfer system, 53

FILTER—
  crankcase, 30
  oil tank, 29
  petrol, 12
Float chamber, inspecting, 18
Foot controls, 4
Footrests, 5
Front forks, replenishing, 69, 130
Fuse, live, 58

GEARBOX—
  lubricants, recommended, 35
  topping-up, 33
  trouble, 83
Gear-change lever, 5
Greases, recommended, 39
Grease-gun, use of, 39
Gudgeon-pin removal, 118

HANDLEBARS, 6
Headlamp beam, setting, 60
Headlamps, 58
High-tension pick-up, 46
Horn, 63

IGNITION—
  coils, 50, 57
  cut-out button, 2
  switch, 4, 7, 48, 56

IGNITION (*contd.*)—
 timing, 96–8
Induction manifold, 17, 19

LAMPS, Lucas, 58–61
Lighting switch, 3, 56
Lubrication—
 brake, 39
 chart, 42
 clutch, 35
 contact-breaker, 50, 51
 control levels and cables, 41
 dipper switch, 41
 dynamo, 43, 44
 front forks, 69, 130
 gearbox, 33
 hub bearings, 44
 magneto, 44–5
 oil-bath chain case, 35–8, 84
 overhead rockers, 33
 rear suspension, 40
 secondary chain, 38
 sidecar chassis, 42
 speedometer cable, 41
 steering head, 41
Lucas lighting and ignition, 47–58

MAGNETO maintenance, 44–7
MoT certificate, 9

OIL-bath chain-case cover, 85
Oil—
 changing, engine, 29
  gearbox, 35
 circulation, checking, 28
 pipes, 32
 pressure, gauge, 29
  indicator, 4
  release valve, 30–3
 pump, 25, 32
 recommendations, 28
 tank filter, cleaning, 29
 topping-up, 28

PETROL—
 consumption, excessive, 15
 filter, 12, 19
 tank, removing, 99, 103, 106
 taps, 6
Pillion passenger, 77
Pilot, bulb, 59
 jet, obstructed, 15

Pipes, oil, 32
Piston—
 removal, 118
 rings, 115–17
Pistons, fitting, 118
 oversize, 117
Primary chain adjustment, 78–80

REAR suspension units, 40, 83
Rectifier, Lucas, 48, 56
Running-in, 8
Rusted parts, easing, 42

SECONDARY chain, 38, 80
Shock-absorber, unit, 84–7
Sidecar—
 attaching, 83
 lubrication, 42
 wheel alignment, 83
Slow-running adjustment, 13, 15, 22
Sparking plugs, 64, 65
Speedometer, 2, 9, 41
Starting engine, 6–8
Steering-head—
 lubrication, 41
 play, 70–2
Stop-tail lamp, 60
"Swinging arm", 40, 81
Synchronizing twin carburettors, 14

TARNISHING, 69
Throttle-valve, inspecting, 18
Tick-over, engine, 13, 22
Timing gear markings, 95, 96
Tyre pressures, recommended, 77

VALVE—
 clearances, 90–4
 spring compressor, 112
 timing, 94–8
Valves, 112–14
Voltage control, automatic, 43

WHEEL—
 alignment, 82–3
 front, balanced, 72, 78
 rear, quickly-detachable, 72–6
 standard, 73–4
Wiring diagrams, 63
Workshop manuals, 120

OTHER TRIUMPH MOTORCYCLE MANUALS CURRENTLY AVAILABLE IN THIS SERIES:

TRIUMPH 1935-1939 MAINTENANCE & REPAIR MANUAL

All Pre-War single & twin cylinder models: L2/1, 2/1, 2/5, 3/1, 3/2, 3/5, 5/1, 5/2, 5/3, 5/4, 5/5, 5/10, 6/1, Tiger 70, Tiger 80, Tiger 90, 2H, Tiger 70C, 3S, 3H, Tiger 80C, 5H, Tiger 90C, 6S, 2HC, 3SC, 5T Speed Twin, 5S and T100 Tiger 100.

Much of the data is applicable to earlier models that utilize the following engines: <u>Single Cylinder:</u> 250cc OHV, 350cc SV, 350cc OHV, 500cc SV, 500cc OHV, 550cc SV and 600cc SV. <u>Twin Cylinder:</u> 500cc OHV and 650cc OHV.   **ISBN: 1-58850-066-7**

TRIUMPH 1937-1951 WORKSHOP MANUAL (A. St. J. Masters)

The most comprehensive Workshop Manual available for pre swing-arm Triumph motorcycles. Covers rigid frame and sprung hub single cylinder SV & OHV and twin cylinder OHV pre-war, military, and post-war models: 2H, Tiger 70, Tiger 70C, 3S, 3H, Tiger 80, Tiger 80C, 5H, Tiger 90, Tiger 90C, 6S, 2HC, 3SC, 5T Speed Twin, 5S, T100 Tiger 100, 3HW, 3SW, 5SW, 3T, Grand Prix, TR5 Trophy and 6T Thunderbird.

Much of the data is applicable to earlier models that utilize the following engines: <u>Single Cylinder:</u> 250cc OHV, 350cc SV, 350cc OHV, 500cc SV, 500cc OHV and 600cc SV. <u>Twin Cylinder:</u> 350cc OHV, 500cc OHV and 650cc OHV.   **ISBN: 1-58850-064-0**

TRIUMPH 1945-1955 FACTORY WORKSHOP MANUAL NO.11

The most comprehensive Workshop Manual available for pre-unit, twin-cylinder Triumph motorcycles. Covers the full line of rigid frame, sprung hub, swing-arm and 350cc models: 5T Speed Twin, T100 Tiger 100, TR5 Trophy, 6T Thunderbird, T110 Tiger 110 and 3T De-Luxe.

Much of the data is applicable to later models that utilize the following engines: Twin Cylinder 350cc OHV, 500cc OHV and 650cc OHV.
ISBN: 1-58850-065-9

~ WWW.VELOCEPRESS.COM ~

OTHER CLASSIC MOTORCYCLE MANUALS CURRENTLY AVAILABLE IN THIS SERIES:

AJS (BOOK OF) ALL MODELS 1955-1965:
350cc & 500cc Singles ~ Models 16, 16S, 18, 18S

ARIEL WORKSHOP MANUAL 1933-1951:
All single, twin & 4 cylinder models

ARIEL (BOOK OF) MAINTENANCE & REPAIR MANUAL 1932-1939:
LF3, LF4, LG, NF3, NF4, NG, OG, VA, VA3, VA4, VB, VF3, VF4, VG, Red Hunter LH, NH, OH, VH & Square Four 4F, 4G, 4H

BMW FACTORY WORKSHOP MANUAL R27, R28:
English, German, French and Spanish text

BMW FACTORY WORKSHOP MANUAL R50, R50S, R60, R69S:
Also includes a supplement for the USA models: R50US, R60US, R69US. English, German, French and Spanish text

BSA PRE-WAR SINGLES & TWINS (BOOK OF) 1936-1939:
All Pre-War single & twin cylinder SV & OHV models through 1939
150cc, 250cc, 350cc, 500cc, 600cc, 750cc & 1,000cc

BSA SINGLES (BOOK OF) 1945-1954:
OHV & SV 250cc, 350cc, 500cc & 600cc, Groups B, C & M

BSA SINGLES (BOOK OF) 1955-1967:
B31, B32, B33, B34 and "Star" B40 & SS90

BSA 250cc SINGLES (BOOK OF) 1954-1970:
B31, B32, B33, B34 and "Star" B40 & SS90

BSA TWINS (BOOK OF) 1948-1962:
All 650cc & 500cc twins

BSA TWINS (SECOND BOOK OF) 1962-1969:
All 650cc & 500cc, A50 & A65 OHV unit construction twins

DUCATI OHC FACTORY WORKSHOP MANUAL:
160 Junior Monza, 250 Monza, 250 GT, 250 Mark 3, 250 Mach 1, 250 SCR & 350 Sebring

HONDA 250 & 305cc FACTORY WORKSHOP MANUAL:
C.72 C.77 CS.72, CS.77, CB.72, CB.77 [HAWK]

HONDA 125 & 150cc FACTORY WORKSHOP MANUAL:
C.92, CS.92, CB.92, C.95 & CA.95

HONDA 90 (BOOK OF) ALL MODELS UP TO 1966:
All 90cc variations including the S90, CM90, C200, S65, Trail 90 & C65 models

HONDA 50cc FACTORY WORKSHOP MANUAL: C.100

HONDA 50cc FACTORY WORKSHOP MANUAL: C.110

HONDA (BOOK OF) MAINTENANCE & REPAIR 1960-1966:
50cc C.100, C.102, C.110 & C.114 ~ 125cc C.92 & CB.92
250cc C.72 & CB.72 ~ 305cc CB.77

LAMBRETTA (BOOK OF) MAINTENANCE & REPAIR:
125 & 150cc, all models up to 1958, except model "48".

LAMBRETTA (SECOND BOOK OF) MAINTENANCE & REPAIR:
125, 150, 175 & 200cc, all Li & TV models and derivates from 1958 to 1970.

NORTON FACTORY TWIN CYLINDER WORKSHOP MANUAL 1957-1970: *Lightweight Twins:* 250cc Jubilee, 350cc Navigator and 400cc Electra and the *Heavyweight Twins:* Model 77, 88, 88SS, 99, 99SS, Sports Special, Manxman, Mercury, Atlas, G15, P11, N15, Ranger (P11A).

NORTON (BOOK OF) MAINTENANCE & REPAIR 1932-1939:
All Pre-War SV, OHV and OHC models: 16H, 16I, 18, 19, 20, 50, 55, ES2, CJ, CSI, International 30 & 40

SUZUKI 200 & 250cc FACTORY WORKSHOP MANUAL:
250cc T20 [X-6 Hustler] ~ 200cc T200 [X-5 Invader & Sting Ray Scrambler]

SUZUKI 250cc FACTORY WORKSHOP MANUAL: 250cc ~ T10

TRIUMPH (BOOK OF) MAINTENANCE & REPAIR 1935-1939:
All Pre-War single & twin cylinder models: L2/1, 2/1, 2/5, 3/1, 3/2, 3/5, 5/1, 5/2, 5/3, 5/4, 5/5, 5/10, 6/1, Tiger 70, 80, 90 & 2H. Tiger 70C, 3S & 3H, Tiger 80C & 5H, Tiger 90C, 6S, 2HC & 3SC, 5T & 5S and T100

TRIUMPH 1937-1951 WORKSHOP MANUAL (A. St. J. Masters):
Covers rigid frame and sprung hub single cylinder SV & OHV and twin cylinder OHV pre-war, military, and post-war models

TRIUMPH 1945-1955 FACTORY WORKSHOP MANUAL NO.11:
Covers pre-unit, twin-cylinder rigid frame, sprung hub, swing-arm and 350cc, 500cc & 650cc.

VELOCETTE (BOOK OF) MAINTENANCE & REPAIR:
Covers LE Mk. I, II, & III, Valiant, Vogue, MOV, MAC, KSS, KTS, Viper, Venom & Thruxton. Includes some limited material on the Viceory scooter

VESPA (BOOK OF) MAINTENANCE & REPAIR 1946-1959:
All 125cc & 150cc models including 42/L2 & Gran Sport

VINCENT WORKSHOP MANUAL 1935-1955:
All Series A, B & C Models

~ WWW.VELOCEPRESS.COM ~

ARE YOU:

INTERESTED IN EUROPEAN, IMPORT & EXOTIC AUTOMOBILES?

DO YOU:

DO YOUR OWN MAINTENANCE?

If you answered yes to either of these questions, then you should check out our automobile books and manuals. We have included a sample listing of some of our featured marques. However, for complete details and the most up-to-date information, please visit our website.

Abarth, Alfa Romeo, Austin Healey,
BMW, Ferrari, Fiat, Jaguar, Land Rover,
Maserati, Mercedes-Benz, MG, Mini,
Morris, Peugeot, Porsche, Renault, Rover,
Sunbeam, Triumph, Volvo, VW.

——— www.VelocePress.com ———

The fastest growing specialist USA publisher of niche market automotive books and manuals.

All VelocePress titles are available through your local independent bookseller, Amazon.com or direct from VelocePress. Wholesale customers may also purchase direct or from the Ingram Book Group.

www.ingramcontent.com/pod-product-compliance
Lightning Source LLC
Chambersburg PA
CBHW070553170426
43201CB00012B/1830